CHOOSE HOPE + CULTIVATE JOY
In the Middle of Life's Most Complicated Seasons

Make Room for
joy

VANESSA JOY WALKER

Carpenter's Son Publishing

Dedication

... for my two moms—Ann and Elsie.

One birthed me from her womb and loved me from a distance. The other birthed me from her soul and loved me upclose. I wouldn't be anything without their combined sacrifices, love, and prayers.

"She is more precious than jewels, and nothing you desire can compare with her."
—Proverbs 3:15

Make Room for Joy
©2020 by Vanessa Joy Walker

Published by Carpenter's Son Publishing, Franklin, Tennessee

Published in association with Larry Carpenter of Christian Book Services, LLC www.christianbookservices.com

Connect with Vanessa about coaching and collaboration at VanessaJoyWalker.com. Or find her on Instagram, Facebook, and LinkedIn @VanessaJoyWalker.

Cover and Interior Design by Adept Content Solutions

Edited by David Brown

Author Photo, AnMon Photography

Cover background images used under license from Shutterstock.com

Printed in the United States of America

978-1-952025-01-3

The contents

Part 1

Getting to Know You

Part 1: Getting to Know You
Becoming Fast Friends

"a sweet friendship refreshes the soul."
—*Proverbs 27:9 (MSG)*

We are about to embark on a journey toward more joy in all aspects of our lives. Are you ready? Just your purchasing this book means that you are already committed to experiencing more joy in your life. I am excited to share with you how no matter what stage of life you are in, joy can always be cultivated and experienced. "Really, Vanessa? Every stage?" Let me start by encouraging you with a resounding YES! Through diagnosis, through a divorce, mourning, and loss. Through it all an abundance of joy is available.

No matter what stage of life you are in, *joy* can always be cultivated and experienced.

The truth is, if we are going to talk about how to have joy amidst pain, then you should be prepared for it to get real deep very quickly. Since we are going to navigate some troubled areas of the human experience, I thought we should become fast friends first. I have kind of an unbelievable story that at times can be difficult to follow, so giving you a road map of my life is necessary if we are to be a close as I'd like! If we were together right now, I would brew you a cup of strong coffee and ask you how you like it—I drink mine black, but because I am a people pleaser (we can talk about that later), I have every necessary coffee accompaniment at my house—just in case. And if you don't drink coffee, then I have tea, all kinds of tea! I also have way too many biscuits to accompany said coffee and tea. (Biscuits = Small sweet cookies that Canadian grandmothers give you with every hot beverage served.) I love coffee and biscuits—especially the chocolate-covered ones. They have seen me through many joy-filled moments and many more difficult times. Coffee and chocolate-covered biscuits increase my **"joy quotient!"** Do you have comfort foods or different ways of cultivating and increasing your own joy? By the way, I came up with the term, 'Joy Quotient' as a way of describing and evaluating my level of joy at any given moment. Learning to recognize how joy is showing up in your life is vital if you are going to be successful at identifying what increases your joy and what attacks or suffocates your joy.

As promised, here is the snapshot of my life:

1975	Abandoned at birth.
	Adopted by the perfect family (which actually wasn't perfect—but what family is?)
1991	Devastated by a betrayal which leads to some severe "church hurt."
1997	Escaped my life to marry the "perfect guy" only to find out no man is perfect—except for Jesus!
2006	Betrayed again. Enough said.
2007	Oh, "Hi, cancer, so nice of you to show up when my whole life is already falling apart!"
2010	Divorced... finally
2011	New beginnings (Met the true love of my life—Lenny Ray—a.k.a. Mr. Walker)
2012	New cancer—What?!
	Babies please! Or maybe not—infertility, IVF, surrogacy, miscarriage...shall I continue?
TODAY	The real blessing. I am still here!

I know that's a lot to take in. When I write it down it feels overwhelming too! Take a moment to regroup and then listen up. While this book may be my story, it is not about me—it's about you. That's right, you heard me correctly. If you are reading this, I want you to know that before I wrote a word, God knew you needed this. It was written with your life, and your experiences in mind. It was written with the purpose and goal of equipping you to increase your own personal "joy quotient" no matter what is going on around you. If you are expecting a straight-up memoir, you will be disappointed. Sure, you are going to learn way more about me and my "stuff" than you'd probably like to know, but my story is just one of many. It is no more important or valid than anyone else's story, including yours. Your story will be exactly what is needed to inspire someone, someday to make a change for the better. Before you bought this book, I prayed for the impact that my story and my experiences could make on your life. Your life and your joy matter just as much as mine do. See, I am not famous. I am not an influencer. I am not an expert. Well, that's not true. I am an expert at something. I am an expert at my own adversity, and I want you to become an expert at yours.

Before we move forward to what I hope will help you to imprint, permanently, God's joy on your heart, you will need to make a decision to be honest with yourself.

> While this book may be my story, it is not about me—it's about you.

Stop for a moment. BREATHE and READ CAREFULLY. You must become intimately acquainted with your own trials and tribulations if you are going to have a say in how you interact with them.

Let me repeat myself! You must become intimately acquainted with your own trials and tribulations if you are going to have a say in how you interact with them.

It is not going to be easy. It hasn't been easy for me, and there are days where it is still tough. I have struggled, cried, yelled, and fought (with everyone, **including God**) all the way to this very moment. And I am still here. The best, most joyful, and impactful elements of life are not a result of the most comfortable journeys. To fully experience the beautiful view at the top of the mountain and the exhilaration that comes from conquering a difficult task, you must faithfully prepare and train to trust that you will make it to the top even when it feels impossible. This expedition of joy is all about building the perseverance to be present in every stage of life. Especially the hard ones.

You must become intimately acquainted with your own trials and tribulations if you are going to have a say in how you interact with them.

I hope that you will stick with me, but more importantly, I hope that you will stick with yourself.

I believe that God has a plan for YOUR story and YOUR journey. You did not pick up this book by mistake, because there are no coincidences. There are surprises, though! God loves a good surprise. I, on the other hand, hate surprises. Seriously. Mostly because I am a control freak, and I think no one plans anything as well as I do (issue number one of one million). Whether you are a seasoned follower of Jesus or your journey has just begun, we can agree that God does everything better. If you just happen to be reading this and you haven't made a decision of faith, I hope you will stick around. God's surprises are guaranteed to exceed our expectations if we are willing to give up the driver's seat and take "the road trip of life" with Him leading the way. You might never write a book, give a TED Talk, or have one hundred thousand followers—or maybe you will! Either way, you are the star of your own story, and I want you to become an expert at your own *God does everything better.* crisis. Why? So that you can become an expert at your own joy. It's all connected. There is a bonus when we become experts at our own crisis: the enemy (that horrible voice inside that tries to extinguish your light) can't use it against you. When this happens, the impact you will have on every part of this world will be changed for the better. I promise you.

It bears repeating because I want you to honestly know that this is not about me. This is about you. This is about you deciding to pull up an extra chair and invite joy to the table. You have the power to increase your joy quotient. Please join me on this journey, and let's step out in faith together.

One more important note. I love exclamation points. I mean, I really love them!!! My editors and friends who think they are editors will probably convince me to remove most of them from the final copy of this book. But now that we are friends, you and I will both know that those exclamation points are secretly there between every line and at the end of most sentences. So many of life's moments are punctuated differently. Instead of ending with a period that lacks joy, let's add some flavor to our world. Let's pepper our lives with the joy that comes with exclamation moments!

I will stop now so that you can begin because I *really* don't want to make this about me!

The Hope of Joy

"The healthiest response to life is joy."
—Mark Twain

Do you have joy? Would someone describe you as joyful?
Would you describe yourself as joyful? Is joy even that important?
I know these questions are not easily answered. Don't worry, I get
it. I have wrestled with the concept of joy in every season of my
life, including while writing this book—about JOY! Have you ever
struggled to define what joy is for you?

Happiness seems to be a more straightforward concept to embrace
and define. I am sure that if I asked you to share what makes you
happy that you could fill many pages with stories of bike rides,
summer adventures, fabulous trips, and other pleasurable activities.
Joy is so much harder to explain. Why? Because joy feels different
than happiness. Joy could be described as that feeling you experience
when you're on top of the world and everything in life appears to be
going your way. Or perhaps it emerges as that unexplainable elation
that floods a room after a baby is born or a long-awaited prayer is
answered. But what does joy look like in the middle of adversity?
Can you feel joy during turmoil and troubled relationships? Or how
does joy show up amidst a major life crisis or devastating diagnosis?

There is no easy answer. Each of us must learn for ourselves what
it means to be joyful when everything looks bleak. It becomes a

Each of us must learn for ourselves what it means to be joyful.

choice. Life has given me many (too many) opportunities to learn about being joyful when things seem hopeless. It took seasons of unimaginable pain and grief for me to be forced into finding true joy. I needed joy to survive—to thrive. For me, it was life or death. Joy is something we choose to make room for and carry with us wherever we are in life. It's not just something you have once in a while when things are going your way and life feels easy. Joy is always there—when you are standing victoriously on top of the mountain and also in the middle of the darkest, coldest night when it feels like sadness and uncertainty might swallow you up in an instant.

When you look at your own life and experiences, do you feel like you actually understand what it means to be joyful? Before you do an intensive and distracting internal deep dive, I advise you to not spend too much time on this question because you might not finish the book!

Joy is complicated, just like life. It is impossible to contain and difficult to describe. It is a sense, a peace, a stillness, a healing balm, a burst, and an energy. Joy is a force that fills in the cracks of brokenness and repairs the damage left in the wake of life's disasters.

Most people have a limited understanding of joy. Early on in life, we are conditioned to focus most of our energy on avoiding anything that might endanger our comfort or happiness (crisis). We exhaust ourselves trying to weave around the natural and unavoidable obstacles of life, leaving little room to learn how to recognize and cultivate joy every day. In addition to that, we are often taught that to experience joy, we must be free from suffering. Conflict and crisis avoidance are modeled for us from such a young age that many of us never learn to see the lessons these experiences can provide because we are too busy running in the opposite direction when they show up.

Joy is a choice and a journey. The version of joy that I've described may sound counterintuitive, but it's real. I've discovered that we can cultivate and maintain joy even in uncertainty. There is

There is room for joy even when our table is full of suffering.

room for joy even when our table is full of suffering. Do you believe me?

It's time to shift the perspective that we have on crisis. Instead of running from it, we need to embrace it, prepare for it, and allow the purpose of each season to reveal itself. When disasters and difficulties erupt, our anxiety increases, and instead of feeling prepared, we panic.

It's time to shift the perspective that we have on crisis.

When you think of adversity and crisis, what comes to mind? Do your palms get sweaty? Does a knot begin to form in your stomach? Do feelings of anxiety and panic rise up? I promise you, you are not alone. I still struggle with anxiety and fear, and pretending that I don't isn't helpful to me or to anyone else.

Trauma, suffering, crisis, disappointment, and struggle are all part of life. And despite what you have been taught, they're actually important—perhaps they are the most essential parts of life. YES, I just said that suffering and everything that comes with it is important and should be valued.

Throughout my shortish life, I've experienced debilitating rejections, betrayals, sufferings, losses, and plenty of grief. Still, I've realized it's because of those struggles that my faith has been strengthened and my purpose more clearly defined. Without those hurdles, I could have never developed the coping skills that now help me get through every tough moment. I was never going to truly embrace joy without fully experiencing sorrow.

How hard do you work to avoid pain? I can probably answer this for you. Humans have proven since the world began that we will avoid pain and loss at all costs. What if I told you that pain is just one of the many keys to sustaining joy? Pain has given me the opportunity and confidence to relate to and encourage others in a more intimate and meaningful way. It is almost impossible to encourage someone if you've never needed encouragement yourself. And you cannot understand suffering if you have not ever suffered.

Suffering continues to remind me that in life, you have two choices. You can either choose hope or remain hopeless. When you choose hope, your circumstances might not change, but the way you live and breathe in them does. When you choose hope and anchor yourself to faith, you can accomplish more than you think you can. Through that realization and that choice, the higher purpose for your life emerges.

Choosing to persevere through pains and trials gives you the authority to speak life into others. That is a gift that I now get to experience. I access that pain from the past, not as a form of looking back but as a way to help others look forward. There is a tremendous amount of hope that you can provide others when they can look at your story and see that each trauma or adversity that you faced didn't defeat you.

We all grow up looking for something to identify with—a label that indicates who we are. We feel more confident when we can say, "I am...(insert your label here)" because it means that we "know" who we are and that we belong. But this isn't always easy. For me, being abandoned at birth and then adopted created its own fractures in my identity and soul. It wasn't as simple as choosing a title or a label. I wasn't just a nerdy kid or someone who loved reading. Growing up, my identity held more questions than answers. I had to create my own labels and also adapt to the ones that were given to me. Plus, they always seemed to be changing. For me, I had a first family and a second family. Both of my families are real, so there is no real family and adopted family here, just family one and family two. Growing up in family two wasn't the fairytale ending that is often depicted in the Hollywood movie versions of adoption. I grew up without many extras, and truth be told, some might have called us poor. I remember the first time I brought a college friend home for dinner and my mom served canned meat. My friend seemed uncomfortable and I couldn't understand why. Didn't everyone eat canned meat regularly? While my parents did a good job making us feel like we had plenty, there was an underlying struggle attached to much of my childhood. My brother also wrestled with his own identity growing up, and my parents had a hard time figuring out how to love and lead a family that was so burdened with brokenness.

Back then, there weren't parenting blogs to help people navigate these difficult moments. It was quite the opposite. Looking back, it was encouraged to cover things up instead of courageously admitting that you needed help. My parents made some mistakes—big ones and little ones. My brother got involved with drugs, my mom was suffering from a mental illness, and my dad—who was a pastor—chose to bury his own pain in an adulterous affair. Many times, I felt like I got lost in the shuffle. The pain of watching my mom go through betrayal ignited a fear-based desire in me to prioritize my search for the security of a manmade savior. What happens when you seek to fill a savior-sized gap with a person instead of God? You make hasty decisions and then wait for the consequences to be revealed. For me, I married young, hoping that it would be what I needed to feel safe and protected from rejection.

Have you ever looked at your parents and swore you would never marry someone like them? I tried to find someone who would be the opposite of what I thought my dad had become. This strategy failed, and I ended up with exactly what I was trying to avoid. Why? I felt like I had a clear picture of what I did and didn't want. The reason my first husband ended up being the wrong guy was that I was looking for someone to save me, and *he* was looking for someone to save. Even though we loved each other, our relationship was built on an uncertain foundation. The results were not good. If we don't learn from generational mistakes, we are doomed to repeat them.

At some point in the middle of trying to save my first marriage and getting cancer, I found myself faced with a new kind of spiritual choice. I could either choose to believe that there was something more significant than me, and it didn't have anything to do with going to church and doing and saying the right things, or I could sit on the floor and accept defeat. And believe me, I did plenty of sitting and lying on the floor feeling defeated.

This was when God began to show himself to me in a new and remarkable way.

I found myself at the same life crossroads that we all eventually face. Standing in the middle of a deserted highway at the intersection of hope and hopelessness. No detours, no maps, and no GPS. What would you do? Choose hope or remain hopeless? When I write this out, it seems like a silly question. I can hear people everywhere saying, "Of course, you are going to choose hope. Why wouldn't you?"

Well, for one thing, choosing hope isn't usually easy. The night before my first cancer surgery, I stood alone, fixated on my naked body in my dimly lit apartment. I felt lost because I had no one to comfort me. I had no one to pray for me. No one was around to hold me tight as I grieved the loss of my unscarred breasts. That night I really wanted to die instead of looking into the ugliness of disaster and deciding to choose hope. I had never felt so alone. Of course, I wasn't entirely alone because God was with me. But in those early moments, the isolation of crisis and my feelings of desperation routinely blocked my view of God. Even so, hope still lingered. A tiny bit of faith was buried deep beneath the pain, and that is what saved me.

Believe me, within each of us is the strength to choose hope even when we are emotionally, physically, and spiritually drained. Strength might build slowly, but even the smallest moves toward hope can bring joy and light into the darkest spaces of despair.

The smallest moves toward hope can bring joy and light into the darkest spaces of despair.

The Choice of Hope

One day, a couple of months after my surgery and right in the middle of chemo treatments, I woke up, and I realized that each day provided a new opportunity for hope; I simply had to choose it. And then tomorrow I'd choose to have hope again. Choosing hope isn't an instant fix. This choice didn't give me the magical ability to erase my suffering. But it did supernaturally change how I seemed to wade through the discomfort. I needed hope to become a part of my daily ritual. Choosing hope would provide me with the ability to experience peace and persevere under enormous pressure. It would also pave the way for joy and healing. The combination of hope and joy was slowly transforming into a beautiful example of God's grace and faithfulness.

Unfortunately, that first cancer diagnosis wouldn't be my last. Remembering the day that I found out that cancer had returned is easy for me. I can still feel the soft yet slightly crunchy paper gown brushing across my minimally scarred body. It had strangely become a familiar and somewhat comforting attire. I was in a good place in my life, and I had moved on from cancer, so I wasn't even entertaining the thought that my doctor might be prepping to delivering another batch of bad news. But I knew the second I saw his face that bad news was coming. Everything changed at that moment. And let me tell you, I was pissed! Guess what? That was okay! It is okay to not understand, and it is okay to be angry.

I felt like my whole body was betraying me all over again. At that moment, I was utterly defeated. Have you ever just wanted to throw in the towel and just let your life implode? I could have given up, and it seemed like the most natural, realistic path to take. It certainly felt easier than standing at that same crossroads *again* with one way leading to quitting and one path requiring me to fight. Honestly, I was so tired of walking either road. In my mind, I was stranded, helpless.

> *It is okay to not understand, and it is okay to be angry.*

Do you see a theme here? Here I was again faced with the decision to choose hope.

I admit this was a hard one. It was a real "But God!" moment in my life. These moments take you from the floor on your knees yelling, "Why, God!" in a moment of complete desperation to being filled with the miraculously ability to tap into that supernatural power and trust that God Himself will sustain you. Consider this a mountaintop moment, just like Moses had when he asked to see God. You are looking in the face of adversity and declaring, "This might look horrible, but God has a plan, and while I can't see past this moment, I trust that He is working it out for my good!"

Take a moment—breathe—and then imagine that you are standing in one of those luxurious hotel rain showers, and instead of water, streams of light are pouring down, saturating you in hope. That is what it was like for me. His strength was definitely made perfect in my weakness. This mountaintop moment was by no means perfect. Doubt and worry still existed here. Trust is a daily choice. During that time, I was tormented with thoughts of death and suicide. I would say to myself, "It would be so much easier if I could just die. Then maybe my story would mean something." Impatience is our natural human response, and to be entirely honest with you (since we are friends now) I didn't want to wait on God for answers. And I certainly wasn't thinking about how I could cultivate joy. **But God!** He was there in the middle of the mess with me. He was keeping me safe and leading the way with just enough light in the darkness to see the next step.

Thankfully, God is not intimidated or swayed by my desperation (or yours). He continued to speak to me. I could feel the peace in my spirit as God said to me, "Trust me, I have more for you. Do you believe me? Will you let me show you?" My doctors were amazing, but their skills and medicines only worked because of hope. Choosing hope is always the first major stop on your journey toward healing and joy.

I wanted to give up, but God wouldn't let me. He had more for me, and He has more for you too!

Why does God let us suffer through heartache, war, illness, and trauma? Because He knows that if we let Him, God can use anything that happens to us (whether that suffering is self-inflicted or an attack from the enemy) for our good. Not just our good, but for the good of others too! What a beautiful truth.

I am not an expert on your crisis, but I am an expert on mine! Through incredible loss, I have learned to choose hope and experience joy in the middle of it. I want you to become an expert on your own crisis so that you, too, can always choose hope and experience joy. I want you to have a sense of peace so beautiful that you are unable to describe it, and an abundant joy so reliable that it doesn't evaporate at the first sign of trouble.

It is time for you to make room for joy, no matter what!

This world is fixated on happiness, which is temporary and fleeting. It is the bandage on our emotional lives, the hard times, and struggles that we will endure, but it is not a complete treatment plan for pain. There is nothing wrong with happiness, but it isn't reliable or sustainable during the most challenging times. Joy is something that we can embrace and experience all the time, especially when it's attached to pain, rooted in God, and fueled by hope.

Joy is something that we can embrace and experience all the time, especially when it's attached to pain, rooted in God, and fueled by hope.

Why should you listen to me? Because I'm still here. It's time to take back the choice of how we feel moment to moment. It is time for us to get intimately acquainted with our pain so that God can propel us toward our purpose. It is time to choose joy, choose hope, and choose faith.

> *It is time to choose joy, choose hope, and choose faith.*

Are you ready to take responsibility for your choice to discover and embrace the joy in every moment? God has the road map and the keys.

Jump in and let's go!

Make It Personal

Is hope a part of your daily ritual? What would it feel like if you were saturated in hope?

———————————— Without judgment for yourself

I challenge you to imagine for moment that you have ALL of the hope in the world! Really though—close your eyes, draw a picture, write down—whatever you need to do to get a clear image of what your life would look like with more than enough hope. **Now check in with yourself.** How are you feeling now? What's standing in your way of experiencing more hope?

What can you do **RIGHT NOW** to soak up a little more hope?

Part 2

Beginnings

Part 2: Beginnings
Defining Suffering

*"To get real about joy,
you must first get real about suffering."*

I love Hallmark movies. I am so obsessed that one of my besties and I will schedule to watch them at the same time so that we can screenshot moments and text them to each other while we are snuggled up watching the movies in different places. She is a big-time PR executive and has also endured her own personal struggles over the years. These "make room for joy moments" help to keep us sane when life and work are overwhelming. My favorite movies are the ones set in small European kingdoms like Moldovia at Christmas time. They always include a regular romantically challenged girl and a handsome prince who is spiraling out of control but needs to find a wife before stepping into the role of king. I know … I can hear your silent judgement, so hush! I also love movies about dogs that get lost in the wilderness and have to fight bears and mountain lions to find their way back to their loving, unrealistically beautiful family who needs them. I don't watch real sports, but I can't get enough of a sports-themed movie. I am strangely always surprised when the underdogs suffer a significant loss, fight back to win the championship, and also fall in love along the way. What attracts us to these kinds of stories? It is hope and the promise of a victorious happy ending. There is nothing better than believing for a brief moment that everything works out in the end and that the journey will only take about ninety-eight minutes.

We've all seen a movie or read a book where the main character goes through something terrible or has a huge obstacle to overcome, and everything works out better than expected. The story is wrapped up neatly with an ending that is so sugary and perfectly orchestrated that we find ourselves wondering what's wrong with our own lives. While there may be a few occasions when things work out this easily, life doesn't typically unfold this way.

Despite what is portrayed in movies or on social media, there's nothing fun about suffering. There's nothing romantic about pain. We live in an age when suffering is too often glamorized or portrayed as some beautiful rite of passage. It isn't. With the ability to share our most personal and intimate moments at the tap of a finger, it is surprising that we are still so averse to full transparency around pain and disappointment. Often, the struggle to create a more palatable and honest narrative turns out to be more debilitating than the original pain itself. I am thankful that there was no Instagram when I was enduring the distress of divorce and the suffering associated with cancer. There were no pictures of me in the hospital when my breasts were cut off and my ovaries removed. There are no snapshots of me curled up late at night with my face pressed against the window of my Brooklyn apartment, waiting and hoping that my then-husband would choose to come home. There are no photographs of my swollen eyes and tear-stained sheets after losing my baby. None of the filters that exist today could wipe away the agony, distress, pain, and misery those pictures would depict.

With the ability to share our most *personal and intimate moments* at the tap of a finger, it is surprising that we are still so *averse* to full transparency around *pain and disappointment.*

To suffer: To submit to or be forced to endure; to endure death, pain, or distress; to sustain loss or damage; to be subjected to disability or handicap.

Distress, misery, and agony all mean the state of being in great trouble.

Distress implies an external, and usually temporary, cause of great physical or mental strain and stress.

Suffering is a conscious endurance of pain or distress.

Misery stresses the unhappiness, especially in sickness, poverty, or loss.

Agony suggests pain too intense to be borne.

—Merriam-Webster

Suffering is a reality and one you will experience from time to time as you live your life. Sometimes it's big, other times it's small. It will arrive dressed up as grief, betrayal, rejection, disappointment, loss, cancer, divorce, or any number of things. The pain can be physical, emotional, and even spiritual. Suffering is a part of life, and while it may be unavoidable, I am waving a flag of hope for you. It's possible to get through suffering without being crippled by it. It is even possible to grow and thrive because of it.

This is why I am obsessed with seeking joy, not only for myself but for you! Do not be fooled; I don't seek joy because I am the most joyful person in the world. If I were, then I wouldn't need to spend so much time thinking about it!

Let's lay some more honest truth on the table. I am sure there are misconceptions about me floating around. People see me at church or on social media and assume that I am a super-exuberant, always happy, and extra-joyful person. But the truth is, the reason why I'm so obsessed with joy is that I have struggled to find it even though I am confident that it is there. Grasping onto joy and allowing myself to experience it has been almost impossible at

The reason why I'm so obsessed with joy is that I have struggled to find it even though I am confident that it is there.

times. Depression, self-hatred, and even death seemed like better options than trying to find some elusive joy in the middle of my broken, crisis-filled life.

Over the years, I've realized that to get real about joy, you have to get real about suffering. And to get real about your purpose, you have to get real about your pain. None of these are easy or fun concepts to become an expert on, but you have to do the work to arrive at the desired destination.

I know it isn't easy to persevere through the hard times. My husband and I have suffered through many things, from cancer to infertility, surrogacy, and miscarriage. We endured the physical, emotional, and spiritual pain of it all. We grew weary in our bodies and in our spirits. There have been plenty of times when I just wanted to give up. You are going to learn a lot about me in the coming chapters, and I don't want to get ahead of myself. But I do want to make it clear that suffering **sucks**. My mom is going to be so mad that I used that descriptive word, but it is true. Cancer is horrible, chemo is the worst, and trying to figure out how to have sex after premature menopause messes with your relationship and your self-esteem. It is incredibly difficult to believe that you are fearfully and wonderfully made when you also know that your ovaries are broken and your cells have mutated in ways that increase your losses and intensify your pain.

Suffering is the uncertainty that overwhelms you when you're in the middle of the dark tunnel. It's the helplessness you experience when you can't seem to see the light at the end of the emptiness. The weight of it presses in on all sides and becomes too heavy to carry. It's the feeling of hopelessness that tries to overtake you when your prayers go unanswered. Suffering is hard to look at, unbearable to feel, and totally unavoidable in this life.

> *Suffering is hard to look at, unbearable to feel, and totally unavoidable in this life.*

I was born into suffering, and I was born out of a crisis.

Forty-some years ago, a young girl was about to give birth to her first child. She found herself at a hospital unwed, without the father of her unborn baby, and about to marry another man who was leading a destructive life. When I picture myself in her shoes, with fear and the overwhelming feeling of failing, I can only assume that she felt trapped and without any other options. She planned to marry this man and keep the baby. But God had already begun to orchestrate something else, a plan that would alter this baby's life forever. I entered this world with the given name Carrie Ann, but that girl only existed for a moment.

See, I am adopted. I know that is a blessing, but at the time, this was a significant loss for everyone involved. My first mom didn't leave with me wrapped in the mint green crocheted blanket that her mom had created for me. She didn't get the chance to take photos with me wearing the pink and white lace onesie that she had planned to carry me home in. I was her first born and all of the firsts that you expect a brand new mommy to experience didn't exist for her. Countless times I have tried to imagine what every single minute was like for her in that small hospital room, knowing that soon she would be forever separated from her sweet girl.

My first mom was probably still in shock when she left the hospital. The clothes that she was wearing didn't matter because no one was waiting at home to capture her picture or record her arrival. The one thing I know for sure is that both of us left that hospital swaddled in grief and unprepared for the suffering that was to follow.

At the same time, just down the street in what seemed like a different world, a young couple was settling into married life and planning for the next stage of their relationship—parenthood. The husband, Mike, was a pastor of a tiny Methodist church, and the wife, Elsie, had left her career as a nurse to fill the roles of a pastor's wife and stay-at-home mom. If you haven't guessed yet, these are my parents—the ones that chose me as their daughter. When Elsie and Mike got married, they had plans for Mike to finish school, find a church, and then start a family. They soon learned that the final step in their plan, starting a family, would not be as easy as they thought. Despite faith and prayer, this couple's parenthood would not be borne out of a natural, joyous, and intimate union. Instead, their journey to having a child would be plagued by each successful pregnancy ending in miscarriage. This was devasting. Elsie routinely fell to her knees in prayer, crying out to God, begging Him to answer her prayer and to give her a child. Nothing happened. She spent many Mother's Days at church greeting the fertile (and what seemed like) more fortunate women with a smile, all the while being tortured by her own disappointment, despair, and feelings of inadequacy.

Have you or someone you love ever faced the hardship of infertility? It is filled with some of the most primitive pains and feelings of failure to envelope a couple. For a woman, the betrayal can be almost unbearable. Acknowledging that our bodies can't do the one thing that they were made for can create a chasm of despair and feelings of inadequacy that the enemy capitalizes on as you struggle to keep the most basic semblance of faith. This is just one example of the kind of suffering that inflicts us throughout life and makes it difficult to believe that anything good could come from such pain. Have you ever been there?

Yet despite the pain and suffering, somehow, in the middle of this mess, God lead Elsie to pray for *her* children, the children that she didn't have yet. She didn't pray that God would choose for her the most beautiful or well-behaved children, but instead, the ones who would need a mom like her. The children whose lives would require a woman who knew how to get on her knees and storm the gates of heaven. The ones who would need a woman who chose to seek God even when life's circumstances made her feel like doing the opposite. She got specific, and God took notice of this humble and obedient woman and chose her for the task of a special kind of motherhood. My brother and I are the answers to that woman's prayers.

When I think about my beginning and my two moms, I am reminded that I had to be abandoned by one mother to be the answer to another mother's prayer. I was the crisis, but I was also the gift. This is just one of many times that I have personally seen God take something that could be destructive and transform it into something amazing.

Mourning and celebration often collide. Life will try to make us choose joy or sadness, but sometimes we must simply choose to grab onto both. I like to think that is why God gave us two hands. You and I need to grab the hand of joy and the hand of sorrow at the same time. There is beauty embedded in this complicated relationship. I still experience sadness for the lost moments between my first mom and me—for every hug, word, and touch that was never shared. Yet I also celebrate the life I see reflected in the mirror—MY life.

Beauty is birthed out of sacrifice and suffering. It really does rise like a phoenix from the ashes of crisis and pain. God has a way of taking the burnt pieces of life—every ash—and transforming them into a higher purpose, one that promises to exceed our expectations and magnify the impact we will have in this world. Beauty thrives within the complicated relationship of joy and sorrow.

> *Beauty is birthed out of sacrifice and suffering.*

At times, I've tried to first push these moments of pain aside instead of leaning into the purpose that surrounds them. It always seems more intuitive to avoid the pain or dismiss it instead of embracing it. It's kind of like when you are totally into someone, and you want them to be into you, but you haven't talked to them yet. There's the torment of the unknown and the uncertainty of how it will all work out. The suffering here is that you are desperate for something to happen, but unsure of how or when it will come to pass. Perhaps you have a dream for a call on your life, but nothing seems to be happening. You are trapped in the waiting room of life. In your hand there's a ticket with your name on it, but unfortunately it never gets called. Instead, you watch everyone step into their purpose, everyone except you.

Thriving requires us to believe deep in our souls that there is an opportunity hidden within every pain.

This is never enjoyable, and you would be a supernatural being if you didn't want the suffering to end. This is why figuring out how to thrive in the middle of suffering is so important. Thriving requires us to believe deep in our souls that there is an opportunity hidden within every pain. The best way I have heard this described is by the remarkable Katherine and Jay Wolfe, a.k.a. "Hope Heals." In their new book, *Suffer Strong*, they dive deeply into the possibilities that exist in the middle of the pain. The phrase "suffer strong" inspires me, normalizes my own journey, and helps me to live everyday more courageously. Suffering does not erase the possibility for joy. It can instead intensify the joy available to you during the struggle. Allowing our minds and hearts to shift toward this truth is vital if we are to thrive. Being unable to cultivate joy amid the tough times leads to increased feelings of depression, anxiety, fear, and hopelessness—believe me, I know because I've been there. Conversely, when you make space for gratitude during these times, focus on gifting grace to yourself, and get excited about the growth that you trust will emerge from this trial, then the purpose of the pain becomes easier to imagine.

> *Suffering does not erase the possibility for joy.*

No one likes suffering, but often we spend so much time trying to avoid it that we limit our own growth and potential. We obsessively read self-help books, go to every inspirational conference, save every motivational post on social media, and buy every "find your joy" journal. We do all of these things in an attempt to prevent or avoid the pain and suffering that might result from a difficult situation. But the truth is that no matter what you do, difficulties still happen. Let me tell you a secret: We do not have total control over every crisis that might come our way. Loss, grief, health challenges, and trials of one kind or another happen to everyone. What if instead of avoiding the pain, we decided to lean into it? EEK ... that sounds uncomfortable, right? The key to finding comfort in this process is to prepare yourself to face it rather than spend all of your energy trying to avoid it. Suffering is going to be a part of your life. It can tear you down, or it can build you up. It's a fight. It's a boxing match. It's a marathon. It's a long hike. The more you train for it, the more likely you are to triumph at the end of it.

God prepares us for suffering by first letting us know that it's going to happen, and then He gives us tools to traverse it with a promise that we will overcome this moment in the end. He promises that something beautiful will rise from the difficulties because each trial strengthens our faith and refines our character. In James 1:2–4, we are told that we should consider it pure joy when we face trials because it will produce perseverance and make us mature so that we will lack nothing. These promises are written in stone and God will deliver. But even though I know in my head that His joy and my pain will be used for good, I don't always feel it in my heart.

Over the years, I've routinely asked God to use my story to help and encourage others. And then, when pain or disappointment hits me in the face, I usually end up yelling, "Why, God? Why me?" He lets me stomp my feet and finish yelling. Then, after my tantrum is over, He speaks, "You know Vanessa, I cannot enlarge your territory and expand your influence if you're not first willing to go to a place of pain yourself. How can you speak to the pain of others if you haven't experienced it? How can you understand suffering if you aren't willing to step into it yourself? Do you trust that I will see you through this? Do you believe that I have a plan?"

Do you remember what I said at the beginning of this chapter? You can't get real about joy if you don't get real about suffering. Joy and suffering are dependent on each other because they were always intended to go hand in hand. A life saturated in joy will transform even the worst of circumstances.

Embracing the truth about suffering, preparing yourself to overcome it, and seeking to learn and grow from it is what makes joy possible. God promises that there is value woven into the process of pain. He promises that the difficulties we endure will strengthen our faith while nurturing a spirit of perseverance within us. I choose to anchor myself to the things of God because His strength has always sustained me. God has plans to use you and your suffering in ways that you can't imagine. A time of suffering is the training ground for a higher purpose.

A life saturated in joy will transform even the worst of circumstances.

Accepting the fact that suffering is a part of life and spending energy preparing to face it doesn't make you a pessimist. Embracing suffering is actually one of the most optimistic outlooks we can have. Why? Because with faith, we can trust that God is going to use whatever happens to us for good. This mindset shift frees you up to experience more joy in each moment because you're not focused on the pain, but on the purpose. You are confident that your joy cannot be stolen because it is a gift that comes from the power of God within you.

We always have access to joy, even in the unpredictable oceans of life. Fear, doubt, unbelief, anger, and bitterness will try to weigh you down, but joy keeps you afloat. The waves may increase, and you may struggle to keep your head above water at first, but joy is the vessel that you can take refuge in. The presence of joy doesn't promise to immediately push the pain or the suffering out of the way, but it does guarantee that you will stay buoyant in the middle of the rising waters rather than be drowned by them.

When I am struggling to see past the pain, I force myself to turn to the promises of God. I remind myself that God has a plan and a purpose that He is working on specifically for me and that every moment of difficulty is strengthening and conditioning me for a journey that will exceed my expectations.

When you believe that you have access to joy in the middle of the suffering, you don't have to worry about getting past it. Suffering helps us experience joy because it provides an opportunity for us to lean into God and all that He promises to do in and with each difficult moment.

"Consider it pure joy, my brothers and sisters, whenever you face trials of many kinds because you know that the testing of your faith produces perseverance. Let perseverance finish its work so that you may be mature and complete, not lacking anything."
—James 1:2-4 (NIV)

Make It Personal

Have you ever been forced to 'get real' with suffering? How has suffering showed up in your life?

—————————————— Without judgment for yourself

I challenge you to finish this sentence: Suffering is …. Be real. Don't sugarcoat your answer and don't compare it to someone else's definition (including mine).

Check in with yourself and take a moment to get curious about how joy could show up in the middle of your suffering.

What can you do **RIGHT NOW** to get real about suffering while still making room for joy today?

Beautifully Complicated

"A complicated life is much easier to maintain and enjoy than a perfectly coiffed one!"

Who can agree that one of the most complicated blessings in life revolves around our families? Those people that we love, embrace, and tolerate all at the same time. Families are beautiful, and I have yet to encounter one that isn't covered in complications.

At the center of my most complicated familial relationships lies my genetics—the family that I share them with and the family that I don't. I have a hard time writing about my biology because it is so complicated—the more I try to make sense of it and understand it, the more restless and confused I become. I used to be obsessed with the "why?" You know, I wanted to know and understand WHY everything happened. WHY was I abandoned? WHY did my God choose to put me in a different family?

WHY does my second mom struggle with mental illness? WHY is my generalized anxiety a constant thorn in my side? WHY did I get cancer when everyone else in my life was building their careers and having babies? WHY am I always the sick girl? WHY does life seem so much easier for everyone else? WHY doesn't God answer my prayers? Why, God? Why me? Sound familiar?

There are a few times every year that the complications of my creation seem to resonate more loudly. Many of those moments center on my first mom and my adoption. My first mom was born in February. I didn't know that important date until I was an adult because growing up, I hardly knew anything about the woman who carried me around in her belly for nine months. This is the mother that I never hugged, touched, or held. There are no pictures of me that capture the connection we share. As an adult, I've learned that she staged a sit-in at her high school so that girls could wear pants. I guess you could have called her an activist! My intense feelings around justice and equity indicate that I am clearly her daughter. She was also a caregiver and a helper. As a much-beloved nurse, she dedicated her life to assisting people who were sick but unfortunately couldn't help herself. Her life was complicated, and I was a part of that complication. I was a part of her crisis and the focus of her pain. That's hard to swallow sometimes.

The complications that surround my identity erupted in the summer of my twenty-ninth year. I was getting ready to leave for Boston to go sing—Fun fact: I used to be an opera singer! I'd be gone for about four weeks, so I had some packing to do. I was rushing around that evening when my phone rang. The woman on the other end said, "Hello, is this Vanessa? Did you just put your name on the Canadian Adoption Registry?" I was totally taken aback because I wasn't sure what she was talking about. Then I remembered filling in some information about my adoption on a government website while I was updating my Canadian passport. I answered, "Yes. I guess that I did." The woman replied, "Okay. Great. It turns out that a biological parent and a sibling have been looking for you."

Okay, I need you to take a moment and really grasp the weight of this revelation. Remember, at this point, I had never seen ANYONE who was biologically related to me. The only information that I had about my birth story is what my parents were told when I was adopted and a handful of details that I received when I was eighteen years old. Who I was and where I came from was as vast and unknown as the outer galaxies are to most people.

When I was a young child, I believed that Madonna was my mom. For real though ... I actually thought that she was going to show up at my house one day with her lace stockings and an asymmetrical ponytail and whisk me away. As I grew older, I pieced together my identity with the small bits of info that I had received along the way. I knew I was part Native American; I knew my mom was nineteen when she had me, and I knew that she eventually married the man who was listed as my father. That's it. So just imagine for a moment how very life-changing this was for me.

After an awkward silence, I realized that the woman was asking me to answer a few questions so that she could confirm the match. In Canada, adoption was done through government agencies, and the only way to connect biological families was if both parties registered. Here I was telling this woman that I didn't know the random yet very personal details surrounding my birth.

She quickly realized that it was definitely a match and then asked, "Can I give your biological mother your phone number?" AHH-HHH! What?! This was so crazy. My thoughts were racing too fast for me to catch up, and I hesitantly answered, "Yes, of course." I was nervous and totally unprepared for this reunion. I had not spoken with my parents about this and had a series of confusing questions and thoughts racing through my brain. Everything I knew about who I was and where I came from was about to change.

My life was about to get way more complicated!

A few moments later, my phone rang, and a soft-spoken woman with a kind voice said, "Hello, this is Ann. I am your mother." Woah. Bear with me, because it is challenging for me to come up with words descriptive enough to capture the complexities of this moment. My heart was pounding so loudly that I could barely hear my own thoughts. Tears welled up in my eyes, but there was no sadness inside. Ann and I proceeded to have one of the most surreal and meaningful conversations of my life. I still have the torn envelope that I frantically scribbled on during our conversation. I wanted every word and awkward pause to be seared into my memory forever. The conversation was kind and polite. We asked each other questions and talked about random things that revealed our undeniable connection.

We both suffered from strange skin rashes—she told me to not eat too many strawberries because they might make my skin flare up. At that moment, I wished she'd been there when Bonnie B was making fun of my acne in eighth grade. I imagined for a moment what it would have been like for this mom to wipe away my tears and tell me I was beautiful and loved. It was heartbreaking and heartwarming all at the same time. I learned so much in that two-hour conversation. She loved music, played the accordion, and adored her three children. That's right, I had three younger siblings—one sister and two brothers.

I also learned that my father was not who I thought he was. My biological father didn't actually know that I even existed, and he wasn't Native American—which obviously meant neither was I. Turns out I am half Polish. This makes more sense—and I *have* always loved Polish food! I fantasized many times about this moment and mentally rehearsed a few talking points. Now was my opportunity to let my mom know how much I'd always loved her. I wanted her to understand that she'd always been a part of my life—that my parents did a great job of talking about my adoption in a way that allowed me to ask questions and embrace her, even though I didn't know who she was. My second mom often reminded me what a sacrifice it was for my first mom to let me go and release me into the unknown. I told her that I didn't resent her or hate her for what she did. I still loved her. I always had.

As I hung up the phone that evening, I felt overwhelmed and stunned. I am sure that I was in shock. We chose to limit our contact over the next month until I had an opportunity to discuss everything with my parents in person. I barely had a chance to really consider my own feelings because I was immediately concerned about the feelings of others. What would my second family think of all of this? That, my friend, is a trait that burdens many adoptees. We are so fearful of hurting the people that saved us that we are unable to recognize our own feelings or needs.

The weeks flew by, and I returned from Boston and headed to Canada to talk with my parents. I remember taking a long walk with my mom at our church camp. I can still smell the wet gravel that crunched under our feet as we headed to the bench near the old basketball court. Growing up, we moved all the time, and this was our safe, constant place. I told her the story of what happened, and we laughed and cried. I couldn't tell if she was sad or nervous. She let this moment be about me and said that she'd support me however I wanted to proceed. I've never asked what she was feeling that day. I am not sure why. Perhaps that is a memory that I have decided needs to be all about me. I headed back to NYC, excited about the possibilities of exploring this new part of my family.

A couple of weeks later, I received another call; an unknown yet strangely familiar voice was on the other end. "Hello, Vanessa? Um … this is Louis, your brother. My grandmother said I should call you. Our mom died today." There are moments in life that truly feel like time has stopped. Thoughts flood in, filling the space until they begin to spill over everything. The impact of life-changing moments like this reduce your comprehension capacity to zero. I don't remember anything else about that conversation, but I do remember collapsing after hanging up the phone. An intense and unpredictable wave of grief flooded the space. I was drowning in tears and regret. My whole life, I had secretly wished to come face to face with the women who bore me, and now that dream was gone. I had missed my opportunity to stare into eyes and bury my head in her embrace. Why didn't I go and see her right away? Why didn't I choose to speak with her again on the phone? There were so many questions and no answers. Have you ever profoundly regretted NOT acting?

I couldn't understand why this was happening. I think I spent three days straight in bed. How could I be grieving someone so intensely that I never actually met? The pain was unbearable and impossible to understand. The family—my family—wanted me to come to the funeral. They wanted me to be there when our mother was laid to rest. My immediate answer was—no. The only memory of my biological mother could not be of her lying lifeless in a wooden box surrounded by those who were intimately familiar with the sound of her voice and the warmth of her smile. In an incredible act of love, my parents—the ones who raised me—went in my place. At the time, I couldn't find anything beautiful in this situation, and truthfully, I wasn't looking. I was consumed by guilt, pain, and grief.

Years later, I can reflect on this and see the beauty in every detail of this complicated and devastating situation. I understand that God gifted me a unique opportunity to connect with my first mom only months before her passing. I see that my mom Ann was able to take her last breath knowing that her firstborn child always cherished her and was safe, happy, and loved.

That embarrassing crisis from so many years earlier—that teenage pregnancy—was now being embraced as a beautiful blessing. I know firsthand how life-changing it was for my parents to honor the woman who gave life to their daughter by attending my first mom's funeral and celebrating her legacy. Her complications were the reason they had me. She suffered and sacrificed so they could rejoice and reap the benefits of raising her daughter. The truth is complicated *and* beautiful.

There wasn't an immediate picture-perfect reunion and connection between families. We tried. About six months after our mom's passing, we all met in Canada in the tiny town where everyone but me had grown up. There were lots of tears and some very awkward hugs. We were cordial and polite, but the atmosphere lacked warmth. I wanted to instantly belong in this place that was surrounded by first mom's love and legacy, but I didn't. At least not yet. Grief was blocking the road to a meaningful relationship. Many years would pass before the beauty of these relationships would unravel. Despite the long wait, I can tell you that the pain, uncertainty, and waiting were worth it. There is so much more that I would like to share. But the words that are needed are still being formed in my heart because this part of my beautifully complicated story continues to unfold.

The truth is complicated *and* beautiful.

In February, I celebrate my first mom's birthday. This is a day when mourning and celebration collide. I said this earlier, but it is worth repeating: Life sometimes tries to make us choose joy OR sadness, but often we must decide to hold both the hand of joy and the hand of sorrow at the same time. Beauty miraculously rises from this complex reality.

When I remember the passing of my mom—the one who gave life and then released it into the unknown—I am sad for every moment that did not happen between us, but I also celebrate the life that I see and experience through all those left behind. I know the joy of her life through the eyes of her daughter, sons, grandchildren, and friends whom she will forever be connected to. I celebrate her as I see it reflected in the mirror. I am my mother's daughter. On her birthday, I hold hands with joy and sadness and feel perfectly balanced. Sure, it's complicated, but oh so beautiful.

It's Complicated

When did this phrase take on the negative connotation that it has today? Why doesn't an "it's complicated" status evoke feelings of success, confidence, and contentment? When did the complicated parts of our lives become things that need to be filtered, cleaned up, and apologized for? Do complicated situations mean that joy and contentment are out of reach? Do complications prevent beauty from rising to the surface? Let's really think about it for a moment. Is there anything in your life that is treasured or enjoyable that isn't complicated? I cannot think of one thing that I love or value that is simple. Everything I cherish is entirely and utterly complicated.

Clearly, my family is complicated, but so are my most treasured friendships. In fact, most are layered with many complications. Sometimes it's because we've been through so much together, but often it's because the complicated parts of our lives uniquely unite us. One of the most complicated friendships I have is with my #SistaWifeBestie Ebony—and yes, we have a hashtag! Well, let me tell you, Ms. Ebony did not want anything to do with me when we met. I mean, why would she? We are from entirely different worlds, cultures, ethnicities, and upbringings. Plus, Ebony was not in the habit of making new friends and inviting them into her tiny and well-vetted circle. But this friendship was destined to be! It was orchestrated in the heavens long before either one of us had an opportunity to object. And once God has decided something, good luck changing His mind—just ask Jonah! *(The one from the Bible.)* Jonah might have taken a significant detour in the belly of a whale, but he still ended up exactly where God wanted him to be! Right?

New Friendships + God's Destination = JOY

I met Ebony, a.k.a. Ebo, one night after a choir rehearsal when another friend of mine offered me a ride home with them. We all happened to live in the same neighborhood. Ebo was driving, and I was riding shotgun. She was the perfect captive audience for my always inquisitive nature. I began asking her questions about who she was, why she was in the choir, what she did, what matters to her … I mean all kinds of stuff. I know for a fact that she was not thrilled at this line of questioning. She was not interested in any new friends, especially a white girl from Canada who talked too much! Yet in that very short ride, I realized that Ebo was also a bit fractured, just like me. Sure, her complicated stuff was different than mine, but it manifested itself similarly.

She didn't like change, she had a hard time trusting people, and she wasn't interested in rehashing every detail of her complicated life to satisfy the inquisitive minds of everyone who surrounded her. You see, she too had been through some unimaginable devastating losses. When Ebony was only nineteen years old, her whole world was torn to shreds. The landscape of every future hope and dream was severely altered because of one sad and hate-filled day.

Ebony's mom—the woman who raised her independently and loved her fiercely—died on September 11th. She was working in one of those towers that came crashing down. I have no words to adequately describe the pain, uncertainty, and grief that my friend must have felt on the days following this horrific life-altering event. I see the remnants of her grief pop up from time to time, and even as a bystander, the pain is palatable and hard to swallow. I can only imagine that in the days after September 11, the enormous fiery piles of twisted steel and rubble which filled lower Manhattan must have paled in comparison to the mounting collection of pain and grief which was filling every crevice of Ebony's heart and soul.

I don't remember how I learned about this complicated part of Ebony's life on this short car ride, but I did. I was instantly drawn to her, and not because I was fascinated by the details of her tragedy, but because I felt comforted by the fact that I was not the only one who was banged up and bruised by life.

God has a unique way of bringing people into our lives to put even our worst circumstances into perspective. I am not diminishing the pain that I experienced because of betrayal and cancer. Still, I can see how different and more manageable my obstacles were in comparison to what my friend was forced to face. So as our ride came to an end and I was chatting away, barely leaving room for a breath between questions and statements, Ebony sharply interjected, "By the way, I don't make friends easily." Unphased, I quickly and joyfully responded, "That's okay, I do!" With that, I jumped out of the car, knowing that I had made a new friend.

Ebony was a friend who I didn't have to pretend around and one who could easily understand my mood swings and pain. This friend didn't care about perfection but instead felt comfortable with the complicated. That short car ride home from a church choir rehearsal was the birthplace of a beautifully complicated friendship that would blossom into an intimate familial connection. Are you connecting with others through your painful moments of suffering, or are you still burying the pain? We can't hope to grow through anything by keeping those complicated feelings buried in the most suffocating part of our soul.

My friendship with Ebony is just one of many that are beautifully complicated. Another super-complicated relationship that I am entangled in is the one I share with Mr. Walker. Wondering who Mr. Walker is? He is my other half. If you skimmed the intro, you would have seen my list of qualifications that have made me an expert on my own suffering. That list includes infidelity and divorce. Mr. Walker is the one that stepped into my broken heart and helped me love again when I didn't think it was possible. We will talk more about that later!

The reason I call him Mr. Walker is because that's what his mom calls him, and when you meet him—and I hope you get the opportunity—you will see that it just fits. We, on the other hand, don't *really* fit together! God could not have chosen two more unlikely people to end up together.

There's nothing easy or uncomplicated about my marriage to Mr. Walker—or his marriage to me! Lenny and I are incredibly different. Our ethnicities and cultures play an important role in how we interact with the world and each other. Lenny grew up in a Jamaican household with Grandma Lulu cooking for him, loving him, and disciplining him in a distinct Caribbean manner. When I learned that he had shared a room with his grandmother when they first immigrated to this country, I was horrified. Who would ever make their son share a bedroom with his grandmother? At the time, I knew nothing about what was typical in his familial culture. I later came to realize that this is culturally normal for many people. It's actually quite beautiful to me now. The strength of the relationship that he had with his grandmother is something to be admired and desired. When I watch how easily he relates to the women in his life, I know that much was gained from spending such precious time with Grandma Lulu—a woman with a strong, kind, and humble heart.

I am culturally a Christian Anglo-Saxon pastor's kid from Canada who spent my childhood living in houses that were adjacent to tiny churches. Our home was always filled with visitors and live-in boarders—a.k.a. extended house guests. I grew up with one brother in small towns all over southern Ontario, Canada.

A significant and complicated pain point for Lenny and me is the difference in the way we give and experience encouragement. Lenny grew up in a household where motivation often came in the form of criticism, especially from his father. Because of his upbringing, Lenny learned to encourage through criticism. I grew up in a family that was not like that at all. I had very few real rules and was not often criticized by my parents. Additionally, the repercussions of trauma have been woven into my DNA. This truth affects how I respond to negative situations. It's difficult for me to brush things off and move on when I feel attacked even in the smallest ways. My instinct is to run and retreat. When Lenny and I became serious, this quickly surfaced as a significant issue, and it still is! Even though Lenny intends to encourage me, the experience I often have is feeling discouraged and attacked. That is the impact of his words.

This doesn't mean that my actions don't sometimes warrant criticism. But this kind of critique doesn't strengthen our relationship. It isn't helpful. So how do we move through this embracing the practice of love-filled submission? Sacrifice and grace.

It is out of Lenny's nature to encourage through compliments and words of affirmation. Yet he knows it's what his wife needs. He has to choose to deny what comes naturally to him and do something for the sole purpose of encouraging his wife—of serving the relationship. Alternatively, I must choose to extend grace to him when he fails. He will always be someone who criticizes—expecting that to change completely is not realistic. This is not easy—for either one of us—but it's necessary. When you decide to submit to one another in love, there is less room for destructive criticism, personal attacks, and self-serving attitudes.

Releasing the need to put yourself first and defend yourself allows you to find yourself. Assuming a posture of humility and kindness proves to be one of the most valuable tactics in tackling differences—especially with your life partner! It is in this vulnerable place that the most beautiful parts of you are uncovered and nurtured.

Recently, someone commented that Lenny and I make marriage look easy. Ha! Ideally, marriage is two people submitting themselves to each other in love. It's a series of choices that involve sacrifice, humility, and selflessness.

> *Assuming a posture of humility and kindness proves to be one of the most valuable tactics in tackling differences.*

To make it work, you have to accept that it's not about you—it's about the other person. Marriage works best when both people are seeking to esteem each other higher than themselves. Eeek.... That sounds complicated! "Do nothing from selfishness or empty conceit [through factional motives or strife], but with [an attitude of] humility [being neither arrogant nor self-righteous], regard others as more important than yourselves" (Philippians 2:3, AMP).

There is an opportunity for overflowing beauty and joy when you embrace a grace-filled posture and journey through ALL of life with someone. Sure, there are the happy times and beautiful things to experience—having a family, highlights of going on a trip, buying a house, and celebrating successes—but the most beautiful thing is the one that is hard to describe with words. It's an intimate bond created by submitting to each other in love. And it is totally complicated. My relationship with Mr. Walker is right up there with the most complicated and most beautiful relationships of my life.

So, back to my original question. Why don't we feel good about the status update, "It's complicated" and celebrate the beauty that is embedded in this transparency? It comes back to shifting our perspective on crisis, difficulty, and comfort. The idea that straightforward and uncomplicated should be our goals is continuously reinforced in the world around us. We can carefully curate, filter, and craft the story of our lives through social media and open ourselves up to the never-ending barrage of perfected life pictures that consciously and unconsciously shape what we think is beautiful, desired, and "normal." Creating what looks perfect online just subjects us to an unattainable view of ourselves and the world around us.

Sometimes in life, we try to uncomplicate things that were meant to be just that—complicated. Why are we so obsessed with finding a neat and tidy answer for everything in life that doesn't seem "right" or feel comfortable? Life is seldom simple. In fact, it usually has several layers of complications. If you wait for things to get uncomplicated before you step into your purpose and choose joy, you will be waiting a long time. When we accept that complications are an essential part of what defines us, then we begin to understand that it's all art. We are all beautifully created, intricate masterpieces.

> *Sometimes in life, we try to uncomplicate things that were meant to be just that—complicated.*

Allowing Change to Happen

We spend too much energy trying to make sense of the complicated parts of our lives instead of looking at them as beautiful pieces of a masterfully written story or an expertly created work of art. Think about the most exquisite man-made wonders in the world—the cathedrals of Europe, the bridges of Brooklyn, or the canals of Venice. If you follow me on Instagram, then know that I am obsessed with travel.

My wanderlust is fueled from a desire to consistently take breaks from environments that are soaked and saturated in grief. Sometimes the best treatment plan for pain is a new environment—one where the air is clearer and the heart is freer. The most beautiful sites I have seen in the world took time and hard work, and they were more than a little complicated to create.

Recently, my mother and I took a trip to Europe, and we had the opportunity to visit some beautiful old churches. In Milan, Italy, we saw the Duomo and actually climbed up into the spires which dot the rooftop of this magnificent place of worship. The Milan Duomo is one of the largest cathedrals in the world. It took nearly six hundred years to complete, is decorated by 3,400 statues, and it took thousands of artisans to build it. Many of the contributing artisans moved their entire families to Milan just to work on the cathedral. They spent their whole lives there working on a piece of art that they would never see finished in their lifetimes. Google some pictures of this cathedral, and you will experience the beauty that is a result of a long, complicated, creative process.

A crisis is full of complications, and you must prepare for disappointment and disaster. You're probably thinking that doesn't sound incredibly inspiring, but understand that I'm not talking about failing to fulfill your purpose or allowing a crisis to steal your hope. I am talking about preparing yourself to face the trials that you will inevitably encounter. It isn't a matter of *if* trials will come, but a question of *when* they will come. There will always be some sort of obstacle or complication. Someone may let you down or maybe you will let someone down. Perhaps you'll get ill or discover you are unable to have children. Male or female, these discoveries can have huge implications. It could be something small or a huge, life-changing event. Whatever it may be, I want to encourage you to prepare yourself to face these challenges, instead of focusing all of your energy on trying to avoid them. Avoiding them will not help you to overcome them or experience joy during them.

It's the complexities of life that allow us to see God more clearly. Nothing compares to experiencing the peace that surpasses all understanding or unspeakable joy in the middle of horrible situations. If someone looked at the last fifteen years of my life, they might conclude that they were the worst fifteen years ever. But the truth is I've experienced the most significant amount of blessings during those difficult years. It turns out that suffering is a springboard for joy because the losses we endure can end up making room for greater blessings. And blessings are definitely beautiful!

Sure, I might be a bit banged up, but I'm still here—and since you are reading this, so are you! I am grateful that we are becoming friends and going through this journey toward joy together.

Suffering is a springboard for joy because the losses we endure can end up making room for greater blessings.

If you are in the middle of a complicated mess right now, let me be the first to say, "Choose hope!" And open yourself up to a broader perspective, one that makes room for complications. The simple act of shifting your perspective on crisis and complications prepares you to embrace them and experience more joy in the middle of them. | *Choose hope!*

"After you have suffered for a little while, the God of all grace, who called you to His eternal glory in Christ, will Himself perfect, confirm, strengthen, and establish you."
1 Peter 5:10 (NASB)

God has built in all the ways that our paths intertwine with others. Isn't it more beautiful to know how things are masterfully orchestrated for our good rather than rely on the simple and tidy outcome we might be able to imagine and arrange for ourselves? What is beautifully complicated about your life? Are you ready to embrace the status, "It's complicated?" Remember, a complicated life is much easier to maintain and enjoy than a perfectly coiffed one!

Make It Personal

Have you ever thought about how the complications of your crises could be used to create a more beautiful and blessed life? What is beautifully complicated about your life?

Without judgment for yourself

I challenge you to think about something in your life that is totally complicated AND unbelievably beautiful. **Now check in** with yourself. What is complicated about this relationship, situation, or crisis? What is beautiful about it? Who might be encouraged by your truth + transparency?

What can you do **RIGHT NOW** to share this complicated beauty with the world?

Discovering Joy

"Joy still exists when happiness ends."

Depending on your upbringing and life experiences, you may think of joy and happiness as the same. Truth be told, they are often viewed as being synonymous or at least closely linked. I want to offer a different perspective, one that is formed on the fundamental belief that joy and happiness are, in fact, vastly different. This became real to me in the middle of one of the most messed-up seasons of my life, and there have been a few!

There are pros and cons for growing up around the things of God. You get a lot of knowledge about the basics of faith and how much God loves you. The downside is that without someone to share their testimony of His love, it is hard to understand. I grew up in and around all things of God and church, but I never completely understood His love for me. I was searching for something else more satisfying to fill me up, and that's when I met my first love.

We both attended a small college in upstate New York and met right before Christmas at an ice cream social. Sounds like the beginning of a perfect Hallmark movie, right? You know that hit the spot for me! I had definitely made some questionable choices in the romance department during my late teens and thought by this point that I knew every single guy on campus. It's a safe bet that I probably dated too much during my first couple of years at college. Have you ever been searching for something, only to figure out that you were looking for the wrong thing all along? When we are looking for something that is NOT God to fill a GOD-sized hole, we will never be fulfilled. I was desperate for attention. I was desperate to feel desired. I was desperate to be loved. Why? Because I had never genuinely learned to love myself. How many of us spend so much of that first part of adulthood just searching for something or someone to give us value? This was going to be a harsh lesson.

> *When we are looking for something that is NOT God to fill a GOD-sized hole, we will never be fulfilled.*

Looking at this stranger, I was pleasantly surprised that I had not, in fact, met everyone. He was tall and boyishly handsome with a hint of drama. There was an instant attraction. He overheard that I had a humanities exam coming up and jumped at the opportunity to help me study. That night at Denny's over french fries and philosophy, he told the waitress that he was going to marry me. I thought, "This guy is crazy!" But secretly, I was totally swept away. I didn't recognize it then, but that rush of adoration was quickly filling up a deep canyon of self-loathing and hurt that had been forming in my soul over many years. We saw each other every day that week before I left for Christmas break. The afternoon of my departure, we met up to say our farewells. As we sat across from each other at my small college apartment–sized kitchen table, I let him know that I was convinced that all guys were only after one thing. I told him not to try and hold my hand or kiss me. If he wanted to pursue me, then he would have to woo me the old-fashioned way—whatever that meant. I left it there and assumed that he would either chase after me or run the other way.

Much to my girlish surprise, he chased! It was the start of what I thought was my perfect love story. That Christmas, we fell in love. I was only twenty years old, but it was real. I loved this boy, and I wanted to spend the rest of my life with him. He had checked every box on the long list that I had been carefully crafting. He was cute, studying to be a minister, and had a God-fearing father who was the perfect role model. His family was precisely what I'd dreamt of having for myself. He was the answer to my prayers. Have you ever thought someone could help you fill the vacancy in your heart or fix what seemed to be broken within your soul? I know somewhere deep in my spirit, I must have believed that he could save me from my past and fill the cracks of inadequacy that were beginning to multiply. Growing up, I was taught that God should be first in my life, but I would give this boy that position in my heart because I didn't trust that God would offer me more.

Betrayal leaves its mark on us all. Being a witness to the marital struggles and later infidelity of my parents created an eagerness to get married and form a better, more functional family. It also led to my early entry into adulthood. I was devastated by the revelation that my father could betray the woman who had sacrificially helped and trusted him through their entire marriage.

A major repercussion of my dad's infidelity was being forced out of our home (which was owned by the tiny church my dad was pastoring) and left virtually homeless. My dad lost his job immediately when the affair was revealed to the church leadership. It is a good thing that as I grew, I didn't base my feelings about the church on the grace and behavior of its parishioners. During that time, I didn't see the grace of God resonating in my faith community. Instead, I was confronted with judgment. What truly impacted me was how that judgment was not all directed at my dad—the one who had done the betraying. Much of it was directed at my mom. This was heartbreaking and confusing. With good intentions, family members tried to force me into forgiveness, using guilt and biblical references as weapons. The impact of these interactions did not inspire reconciliation but instead increased the hurt and anger that I felt toward my dad and toward my community of faith. It was a struggle to witness my loving Christian community treating my mother so carelessly. No one seemed invested or interested in how we were *really* doing. I felt silenced. At sixteen years old, I moved out of my parents' house and started adulthood early. I had always been a daddy's girl. I love my mom, but my dad was the one I held closest to my heart. The hurt of knowing he had betrayed our family just expanded the already existing empty space inside me.

When we are amid trauma, we can't anticipate how our brain and heart will try to protect us and control our emotions. Hindsight is always 20/20. I couldn't see it then, but my vision is crystal clear now. When I met my first love, I was looking to be saved. Frantically running away from pain, betrayal, and rejection, I thought that I could find peace, rest, and happiness in the arms of a man. Looking at it through the eyes of experience, expecting my first husband to save and complete me was unrealistic. You can't argue with the heart of someone too lost to see reason.

I would keep this boy first in my heart and my life because God could not be trusted. I looked at the example of my mom and dad. A shattered family. This young man became my everything—the source of my joy and the dictator of my peace.

My World Turned Upside Down

Ignorance really is bliss. I thought that I had created a happy home with a happy marriage. I was blind to how far behind my husband had fallen, not only in our marriage but also in his faith. When you have no idea that complete devastation is coming, it hits you in the face like a Mack truck. I wasn't prepared at all.

Eight years of marriage changed in the blink of an eye with a conversation I never expected and words that would change everything forever. Have you ever had a life-changing conversation that you weren't ready for? What in your life changed that day? For me, my husband looked me in the eye and said these words to me.

"I love you. You're my best friend, but I don't want to be a Christian anymore, and I don't want to be married."

It felt like a movie. Everything stood still. It was like all of a sudden, the environment was too dark and too light at the same time. Everything was too quiet and too loud. I couldn't see or hear anything clearly. Add to this the sensation of everything pressing in on you and there not being enough air to breathe. My thoughts were racing, and I had trouble even grasping which ones to latch onto.

"This can't be happening. This is not part of my plan. This is not part of God's plan for my life."

His startling revelation came with an immediate change. As if for the last eight years he had been desperately waiting to share with me who he really was.

His honest confession came with a complete change in character. Faithful and God-fearing before, my then-husband proceeded to lie, cheat, and betray all that we had promised each other. His love of the world and his own search for happiness would replace his love for God and for me. The respect he had for me was now gone. His personality did a complete 180. He would say things to me and about me that to this day sting like a fresh wound. "You are sexually unattractive," "You are easy to lie to," and "You need to leave New York City because you will never find anyone here to love you." Anger, bitterness, and fear covered me like a heavy wet blanket on an icy winter's day. Desperation and darkness settled into every part of my being.

I was stunned. I didn't know what to do or where things had gone so wrong. I began to think, "God, what is going on? How could you let this happen?"

The man that once called me multiple times a day to check in began to stay out to the wee hours of the mornings. I never knew where he was, who he was with, or when he would be home. I could tell he was drinking more than usual, and when he looked at me, there was an emptiness in his stare. He stopped touching me, kissing me, and holding me. When you have already lost it all, you begin to look for desperate ways to save any part of what you had before. Sex became a tool that I would use to try and lure him back into communion with me. But there was nothing pleasurable about our intimacy. He had stopped treating me like a wife and started to treat me like a whore.

I know those are strong words, and I hesitated before writing them because of fear that my ex might read this someday. It isn't my intention to hurt him or those that he loves. Everyone makes mistakes, and what happened during that time in our lives does not need to define how he decides to love now. I also don't want to leave out something that could benefit you in your healing process. Even though I have forgiven and let go of this part of my past, at times the pain of divorce still lingers. Have you ever experienced this type of lingering conflict or pain in your life?

When I wasn't trying to use sex as a tool for reconciliation, I would fall into the pattern of self-righteous assaults. I would remind my husband that he was being a bad Christian and that God would punish him for his behavior—this is not a tactic that I suggest. His physical retreat mirrored the spiritual and emotional disengagement that was also taking place. About now, you are probably thinking that there must have been some signs that this was going to happen. This could not have been a complete surprise. And you are correct. As I reflect on this period of life, it is much easier for me to see how this happened. I can now identify the signs that were there all along. Even when we were dating and engaged, my first husband struggled with commitment. He seemed to be drawn to the women and environments that were more exciting than a fully committed Christian girlfriend or wife. I remember him telling me once while we were engaged that he kissed a girl that he worked with at a local restaurant. I was devasted, but so desperate to be loved that I didn't push him to figure out WHY he made that choice.

He started lying to me about little things early on, but I chose to minimize the importance of this and instead sought to make myself more desirable and fun in the hopes that he would continue to choose me. I had committed to this relationship, and I couldn't bear to think about one day being discarded. I did not know that I was enough on my own. I did not believe that I was beautiful and worthy of unconditional love from a man. I couldn't see what was happening because I didn't want to see it. If our marriage wasn't working, if he didn't love me, then those negative internal voices which had battered me for years would be right. I would know that I was disposable, unloved, and undesired. The truth is we had not been in a God-centered marriage for a long time. We had systematically compartmentalized our faith and surrounded ourselves with people who didn't value our understanding of the covenant of marriage. This is the messy truth.

Listen, when you turn your back on God and those He has entrusted to you, be prepared for things to take a sharp detour. What you once were is not what you will become, and it's certainly not God's plan for your life. Your trajectory will change, and the outcome will no longer have the guarantee of peace, joy, and inner prosperity.

Through a period of about four years, I cried out to God. I mean, I wailed! There were no formulated prayers here; it was straight-up wrestling with this God who was supposed to love me. I started to ask Him questions that I had never asked before, and I began to experience Him in ways that are difficult to articulate. The more I fought and wrestled with God, the tighter He held on. It's kind of like when a parent cradles an overtired screaming child. At some point, their weak body gives in to the comfort, and sweet, peaceful sleep takes over. Near the beginning of this journey, God spoke to me, "This is not just about your husband. This is about you. This is your journey too. This is about you learning to hear me, feel me, and experience me in ways that you never have before."

It was right about that time that I picked up a book by Henri Nouwen that ironically belonged to my then-husband. The author wrote about joy in a way that made it seem so accessible, and it got me thinking. He wrote about how joy is not the same thing as happiness.

"Joy is not the same as happiness. We can be unhappy about many things, but joy can still be there because it comes from the knowledge of God's love for us. . . . Joy does not simply happen to us. We have to choose joy and keep choosing it every day. It is a choice based on the knowledge that we belong to God and have found in God our refuge and our safety and that nothing, not even death, can take God away from us."
—Henri Nouwen, Here and Now.

That was the first time I had thought about joy and happiness as being two different experiences. Growing up in church, I routinely heard the word joy, but in many ways, I did equate joy with happiness. I knew what it was like to be happy and unhappy. But did I truly know what joy was? How does joy feel in comparison to the much sought after happiness?

Nouwen states that joy does not just happen to us. We have to choose joy and keep choosing it every day. It's a choice based on the knowledge that we belong to God. It's knowing that God is our refuge, our safety, and our strength and that nothing, not even death, can take God from us. There is nothing on this earth that can snatch us from his hands. This realization was comforting because, at that point, I felt like almost everything had been stolen from me. I believed that I was never going to be happy or loved again.

Losing a marriage is hard. Losing a marriage that you thought was based on fidelity and trust is brutal. The disintegration of my first marriage and learning to let go of the person I had charged with fixing me was indescribably devastating. But God! He can take anything and use it for good.

Hard Lessons

One of the best discoveries from that season was the revelation that happiness has an expiration date. It's an experience that has a beginning, a middle, and an end. I knew I wasn't happy, and I couldn't even imagine being happy anytime soon. The painful rejection I was experiencing exhausted my soul. It was hard to breathe and function. I was embarrassed and humiliated. The harsh and harmful words of a man whom I had given my whole life to echoed in the empty void that his betrayal created. If I was being totally honest, he just pulled the scab off a wound that had refused to heal. It's a dark moment when you realize that your current situation might push you to death. To some, this may sound melodramatic, but for me, this was a critical moment. I needed to make a choice about how I was going to live.

Happiness was out of the question, but I knew that something had to change or I would not survive. Perhaps joy was the answer.

Could joy be experienced in the middle of this craziness? Was it available and in reach when my heart was crushed and my faith almost nonexistent? Was God even real? Perhaps my then-husband was correct—maybe I was too religious and too "good." Maybe my attachment to my faith was doing more harm than good? These were challenging, life-changing questions I was asking myself. Have you hit bottom only to find yourself confronted by the lies and the pain that life has built into you? This is when you have to fight for life instead of giving into death. So many people die by suicide every year, buried in pain and suffering. We must seek to find answers beyond ourselves. Then we will discover the beginning of a new journey that will continue to be painful but will eventually trade emptiness for joy.

I said it early on, but it bears repeating. To get real about joy, you have to get real about suffering. To get real about strong and sustainable joy, you also have to get real about God. It is impossible to cultivate joy when you are not connected to the ultimate power source. Sometimes it feels like my joy has evaporated. It's like I have momentary amnesia and forget who God is and who I am in Him. I let the details of my circumstances become the focal point and forget to look up. Truthfully (because I am so dramatic), I sometimes choose not to look up because it seems more natural and comfortable to dwell in fear than embrace faith and experience the exciting surprise of joy.

To get real about strong and sustainable joy, you also have to get real about God.

Joy takes courage and boldness, and choosing it involves stepping into the unknown. Giving in to joy during the darkest moments unleashes a transformational power that can provide sustainable strength when you are at your weakest. This is a strength that the enemy doesn't want you to tap into, and truthfully, our culture hasn't made it easy to differentiate between joy and happiness.

Why do we choose to stay in fear when we have the promise of joy? It comes down to the misunderstanding that happiness and joy are interchangeable. It's understandable why people get confused about happiness and joy. Happiness is defined more easily, and most people can readily tell you what makes them happy. We have already determined that I love coffee and exclamation points! Both of these things make me happy. Joy is not quite as easy to define. Where happiness is an emotion, joy is more like a knowing. Joy is the quiet moment of peace in the middle of grief. Joy is the indescribable feeling of strength that is rooted and anchored in an unchanging God who loves everyone all the time. Joy is reliable and tempered. Joy is always fresh and never-ending. It saturates and replenishes you. Joy is overflowing and jubilant, but also quiet and consistent. Joy is one of those things that the more you choose it, the more there is to hold on to. The more you share it, the more there is to give. Happiness relies on external stimulus, but joy originates from within. Joy is what exists when happiness ends.

It can be hard to imagine that JOY exists in the middle of the storm, such as during cancer, loss, death, financial struggle, and infertility—during the times in our life when a direction is lacking and our purpose seems unclear. Yet even in the darkest hours when there appears to be no light—God is there. And where God is, joy lives. I used to think that joy was something you had to chase after and grasp on to using your own might. But I have come to realize that by merely choosing HIM—turning to God—joy is not only in reach, but totally activated. **When you choose God, you choose JOY.** You become the light in the middle of the darkness because He is alive and active in you.

Joy is one of those things that the more you choose it, the more there is to hold on to.

Deciding to choose joy every day before the storm hits is imperative because every day is different and we can never predict what trials it may hold. Imagine for just a moment what life would be like if you knew that in the center of your being, there was nothing that could steal your joy? How differently might you approach difficult situations or difficult people if you trusted that no matter how bad things got, you would always have access to a joy that promises to sustain and satiate? Every day has its own set of challenges, but when the joy of the Lord is in you, then you are strong.

Deciding to choose joy every day before the storm hits is imperative because every day is different and we can never predict what trials it may hold.

Happiness is great, but it is an emotional reaction to a man-made experience. I am not saying that happiness has no place. It is a wonderful emotion that is based on momentary feelings. Joy is supernatural and spirit fed, aligned with God's love for you, and is therefore sustainable through life's challenges and difficulties. Happiness isn't something that is easily shared with another person, but joy is contagious. It's something that changes not only you but also your environment and the people who are in your environment.

Joy is indestructible because it comes through God and is from God. When embraced, it proves to be stronger than your emotions, which can take you on a never-ending roller coaster ride. Believe me, I know. I am an expert on emotional outbursts and extreme moodiness. Being stuck in the defeated, victim-based mentality usually indicates that my vertical connection has been compromised and it is time to tap into the joy of the Lord.

Joy is a gift from God that promises to satisfy during times of feast and times of famine. Joy is a perspective. It's a way to reframe everything that's going on in your life. Joy is always available with no beginning or end, but it is a choice. When you embrace God's love and power and place your hope in Him, joy is the natural result.

"Don't be dejected and sad,
for the joy of the Lord is your strength!"
—Nehemiah 8:10 (NLT)

Make It Personal

Where do you think joy comes from? Have you ever thought about the difference between joy and happiness? Have you ever felt like joy wasn't accessible or attainable?

Without judgment for yourself

I challenge you to finish this sentence: Joy is …. Be real and don't compare it to someone else's definition (including mine). Remember, this is YOUR definition for today and it can change tomorrow—joy is complicated and not easy to define.

Now check in with yourself. What's your **joy quotient** today? What is preventing you from making room for more joy at your table?

What can you do **RIGHT NOW** to serve up a larger portion of joy to yourself and everyone else around you as well?

Part 3

Reality Check

Great Expectations

*"And now, Lord, for what do I expectantly wait?
My hope [my confident expectation] is in You."*
Psalm 39:7 (AMP)

Have you ever thought about what you expect out of life?
I sure have.

How about what you expect from yourself?

Questions like these always seem to lead toward more and more questions until suddenly, you are anxious and overwhelmed.

Where do these expectations come from, what are you basing them on, and how have they been formed? Are they even realistic? Are they helping to increase your joy quotient, or are they creating more stress, disappointment, and feelings of inadequacy? Are they taking you down the path of helplessness or hopefulness?

You ever feel like the questioning never ends? I am exhausted already!

These are the kinds of rapid-fire questions that have rattled around in my brain for many years. As I am sure that you can relate. The questioning is especially strong during times of crisis. Numerous times crisis has caused me to stop, regroup, and then pivot my desires and dreams. Difficulties routinely disrupt our mindsets, fracture the foundations of our belief systems, and force us to reevaluate our expectations.

Difficulties routinely disrupt our mindsets, fracture the foundations of our belief systems, and force us to reevaluate our expectations.

Whether in business or in my personal life, I have found that setting the expectations before any project or conversation is invaluable. I try to communicate to those in my circle that if they set my expectations before any event, meeting, or difficult situation, then the result of that event will prove to be more productive and positive. Planning is a way of life for me! The control freak in me requires it, and it is something that, in my life, there is no recovery from. If you or anyone you know has control issues, you understand this better than most.

As with anything in our life that creates strongholds or blind spots, the first step is acknowledging the truth. I have to be 100% honest with myself about my need to have control. Recognizing how I manage and interact with the world helps set the expectations of the people around me. Why is this important? When you know who you are, and you know your triggers, you can expect them, and instead of a terrible surprise, you, instead, know how to shift. Being intimately acquainted with this part of who I am and knowing that it will surface from time to time, makes expectations this planner's best friend!

Now, this isn't a perfect system. Sometimes the elaborate agendas that I craft for myself in my head or heart are not realistic or even the best path to follow. But to figure that out, I need my partners—my people, my teammates—to listen to my expectations and then reset them by responding with their own equally valuable ideas and feelings. "But Vanessa, I am a huge introvert. I don't want to surround myself with people. I can do this on my own." There are going to be times where you think this is true. It isn't. We were created for community. I discovered the value of this skill after years of working with high-achieving, creative, and empowered individuals. I realized early on that if I was to be successful and ultimately be of value, while protecting my sanity, then listening intently to requests and visions and learning to set people's expectations around what I could realistically offer or contribute was imperative. I couldn't be trusted to decide how much was too much. I needed those people around me to help me see what was reasonable and what was not.

Before I started doing this, I was always stressed and overwhelmed. It felt like I was failing more often than I was succeeding. This process of setting people's expectations served both my own well-being and the people I was supporting. It created trust and unity. It also allowed us to believe in each other and feel like we were truly on the same team.

This works in all kinds of relationships. I routinely set Mr. Walker's expectations and communicate to him what I can and cannot accomplish. If this doesn't work for him, then we can chat about it. I can ask him, "What are your expectations of me regarding this situation?" And then I can honestly let him know if I can meet them. When Lenny—a.k.a. Mr. Walker—and I got engaged. I quickly realized that our styles of day-to-day living was remarkably different from each other. We are not cut from the same cloth! Lenny is regimented, organized, and extremely particular. I'm creative, dramatic, and a bit scattered. Many people who know me as an adult make the assumption that I am a naturally organized and task-oriented person. But those are skills that I have cultivated later in life out of necessity. I am sure that since you have made it this far, you realize that I am naturally scattered and dramatic; I'm actually the type of person who doesn't understand why Tupperware needs to be organized! Can someone please tell me why all the lids need to go together? It feels restrictive and unnatural to have to put something back in the same place continually. Mr. Walker is the exact opposite.

This might seem like a small thing. But in everyday life, it's often the layering of small differences that creates disagreement and distance in our relationships. I assure you this is an issue we've undoubtedly had to work on. Tackling it doesn't involve defending our positions or advocating for ourselves. Instead, it means actively listening and intentionally observing what makes each other most comfortable. And then do our best to submit to the other person in love and adequately set each other's expectations. I am not always going to put things back where they belong. That is just a fact. If Mr. Walker is expecting that result, he will routinely be disappointed. This situation requires me to make a real effort and to put the lids in their designated spots and requires Lenny to react graciously with love when I fail. (Because I fail all the time!) This is not easy—for either one of us—but it's necessary if we are going to stay married.

Choosing Hope

People often ask me how I have continued to be sane, choose hope, and live a somewhat peaceful life in the wake of the devastating tidal waves which seem to always fall on the shores of my life. With the sensitivity to faith-based conversations, there was a time when I would try to leave my faith out of my answer. The problem with that is I am not telling the whole truth. Truly the peace that I have received and the joy that I have chosen to experience in some of the hardest times of my life cannot be adequately explained without it! I am not setting the listener up for success. I am not giving them all of the information so that they can then make their own decisions about life, faith, and crisis.

I want to take a moment to clarify a few things so that you can set your expectations about our continued journey toward more joy.

I am a person of faith. I am a Christian and I have a personal relationship with Jesus Christ. My journey is unique, just like yours. The fact that we are both still here means we believe in something. When I started sharing my story more intentionally and with full honesty, I received feedback from a variety of sources. Not all of the well-meaning advice served me and my calling. I was told by some that I should tone down the faith part of my story to make it more widely relatable and to make me more marketable as a speaker and leader in the world of adversity coaching. For a short period, I took that advice. I have plenty of practical tips and stories that I can tell people about all kinds of subjects. I can quickly draw on my personal experiences to discuss cancer care, chemo treatments, divorce proceedings, adoption issues, infertility woes, et cetera. But many people can offer this guidance, and probably more effectively and efficiently than me. We are all unique and have something to offer, and we are all experts at something. The real impact of my journey rests in the fact that I am a person of faith. That is the key ingredient in the recipe of why I am still here.

Remember, this book is not about me. It is about you. We may not share the same faith tradition, and that is okay. My intention is not to convince you that how I operate is the only way, but instead to be transparent about what has helped to keep me functioning and alive for the past forty-four years. My goal is to share with you why joy is so important to me and how making room for it has been the key to finding more peace and satisfaction out of every area of my life. My story cannot be separated from my faith because I am my faith. I am what I believe, and so are you.

To persevere and make the transition from survivor to thriver, you must believe in something. So as you continue with me on this journey toward joy, I ask you to consider: What do you believe in? What or who do you have faith in? Where are you placing your hope? Do you even have hope? What drives you? More importantly, what is your expectation of God?

> *I am what I believe, and so are you.*

The world is full of never-ending updates, and I hate updates. I know hate is a strong word, but I *really* don't like change. It stresses me out. It messes with my control issues! I'd like to think that I am not the only one who breaks a sweat when that notification pops up on my computer—Update Now … or else. I am not saying that progress is a bad thing; in fact, it is vital for growth. But there are not many stable, unchanging things in this world that one can truly trust. In order to move with grace, joy, and peace through an ever-changing world, it is essential to find something or someone who is reliable to place your hope in.

Location, Location, Location

Where have you tried to place your hope? I have tried to place my hope in things, people, jobs, loved ones, and even myself—it never ends up well. At some point, we all fail. Failure is inevitable, and I must tell you something: You can trust me to always tell you the truth and own up to my mistakes, but I will disappoint you. I am loyal, quirky, and kind. But please do not put your hope in me! I am not that stable! Are you?

But God—He is the beginning and the end, never changing, always the same—yesterday, today, and forever. Please learn from my mistakes. I spent many years wading through severe pain that was not due to illness but instead the result of the debilitating disappointment that stemmed from placing my hope in something that was not stable. Building foundations on shifting sand instead of the solid rock of God. I was expecting comfort, peace, and joy from places and people who were not capable of providing me what I needed to survive. The disappointment was more than I could bear.

When it comes to God, He has done an excellent job of setting our expectations on what we can expect from both Him and life. There is no mystery. Just a clear picture that we can depend on.

God is clear about the trials, troubles, and turmoil that we should expect to encounter. He also promises to never leave us or forsake us. God promises to infuse us with supernatural strength in seasons of weakness. He assures us that we are loved—no matter what. And that nothing—that's right, NOTHING—can separate us from His love. This is unfailing love. It is kind, unwavering, never judgmental, and always patient. It is a love that always trusts, protects, and perseveres. God's love promises to never fail.

"Love is patient, love is kind. It does not envy, it does not boast, it is not proud. It does not dishonor others, it is not self-seeking, it is not easily angered, it keeps no record of wrongs. Love does not delight in evil but rejoices with the truth. It always protects, always trusts, always hopes, always perseveres. Love never fails."
—1 Corinthians 13:4-8 (NIV)

My favorite word in the "love passage" is perseveres, because that is what God has done for me. He has equipped me to persevere through the fires of betrayal and the storms of suffering. In God's word, it is called the refiner's fire. Do you know what the refiner's fire is?

In the third chapter of Malachi, God is described as "a refiner and purifier of silver." When you research the process of refining silver, you learn that to remove the impurities, the silver must be superheated (yes, that is a word!) so that everything that doesn't belong is burned away. This is important because when you are refining silver, the refiner must remain with the silver at all times. If he isn't diligent during the process, the silver could be damaged or even destroyed. I want you to think of yourself as that same silver. God uses the fires that come up in our lives as a way to purify us, and He doesn't just leave us and come back when the work is done. He stays with us always. Do you know how the refiner can tell that the silver is ready, complete, and lacking nothing? He knows the process of purifying is finished when he sees his own image reflected in the silver. What a beautiful picture that is of what God does for us! Troubles may come, but I can rest assured that when He is finished, Christ will be more reflected in me. Amen!

There's been no temperature too extreme to destroy me or to steal my joy! I am the result of God's persevering love.

When your expectations are based on trusting and believing in the things of God, you are setting yourself up for success.

Now some of you may have grown up in church and others may have not. For me, growing up in church didn't prevent me from basing my own expectations on what I saw around me. I had expectations about what kind of parents I should have, how I should be treated, and what type of man I would marry. When it came to my first husband, I'd set some clear expectations for myself and for God. For years, I watched my parents' marriage suffer due to infidelity. I observed and experienced the shame my family endured from the church. My mom suffered in silence because no one told her that she had the right to speak her truth and ask for more help. This drove me to look for an earthly savior.

So, I set my expectations on finding a man who was funny, charismatic, and would satisfy my need for a little bit of drama.

I wanted him to have all of the things that I felt I didn't have from my current family situation. Have you ever just wanted to find someone who could fit into your man-made box and fix all the things you felt were missing from your world? I did. And I found someone who (at the time) checked all the right boxes. The problem with those expectations I had created was the lack of spirit-driven guidance when I created them. My wounds were so deep that I allowed this person to become the most important part of my life. I looked to the relationship and to the man to create my happiness and peace. My self-induced expectations not only put unrealistic expectations on my husband but also on myself. Expectations like cultivating happiness and joy for my partner. The codependency of this relationship was comfortable, and for a time, it was predictable. But it was never entirely stable. Unresolved fear follows you, and I had been afraid from the moment that my dad hurt my mom and broke his promise to be faithful. I always feared that my then-husband would be unfaithful to me. Way deep down, I thought the same thing would happen to me. I did all of the "right" things when I got married the first time. We went to counseling, waited until we got married to have sex, prayed, and didn't live together. But in the end, he still cheated on me and treated me even worse than my dad had treated my mom. Despite everything I had done to prepare, the crisis still happened.

Spending all of your energy trying to avoid a crisis, instead of living by faith and preparing to tackle the crisis, is not a wise action plan. Can you imagine, just for a moment, what it would feel like if your expectations could be transformed because of your relationship with God? What would that look like to you? I'm not going to pretend that it's an easy thing to do. I still struggle with this all the time. But when your expectations align with God, there is greater access to peace and joy. When we create expectations ourselves, they are often rigid and in need of deliverables. We need deadlines and timelines that make sense. But who honestly understands God? I sure don't. Thankfully, God's ways are not our ways. Life events aren't all laid out in advance, and there's no weekly schedule that allows you to plan for every eventuality. With God as your travel mate, you begin to understand that choosing to have hope in Him is actually the best preparation for any challenge that might get in your way.

When you're hurt, confused, or angry, you can hold on to the fact that God has a plan to guide you and then allow Him to shift your perspective to the rest in the eternal realm. This is the birthplace of peace. God wants you to strive to become as familiar with Him as He is with you. Remember, "To get real about joy, you have to get real about God!"

To get real about joy, you have to get real about God!

Sometimes it takes hard times to push you into a place where ambitiously seeking God and what He wants for your life becomes the best option. When my ex-husband told me that he didn't want to be married to me, I was devastated. I had checked all the "right" boxes, yet it still came crashing down. I could have stayed focused on the offense and how he had treated me, but the truth is that much of what happened in our relationship was God wanting more of me for Himself. I am not saying that God made my ex-husband cheat and treat me poorly. That was definitely his choice. What I am saying is that it was a complicated codependent relationship that could have only survived if we both wanted to dig in and work together to realign ourselves with God and each other. I could not save the marriage on my own. You could sit down with your spouse and both agree to work it out, and you could both be praying that God moves mountains for you. Just don't be surprised if you wake up next to a shovel because you both will still need to do the work.

Godly Alignment

God used this time to show me what was possible if I decided to align myself more closely with Him. God was saying, "I want you to choose me, and not because it's what your parents told you, or because that is what your religious upbringing has dictated and you know the right words to recite. I want you to know that I am real and that you have access to me. I am the beginning and the end. I know every twist, turn, and detour that the future holds. I am the stability, love, and the guidance that you seek. I am reliable, and I will never fail you." Trust me, when your feet are firmly planted in faith, you may sway back and forth a little, but you are not going to be moved.

Gently, God was pressing my shattered heart back together. Little by little, day by day. He was teaching me to keep my eyes on Him. God was showing me how to be obedient to the still small voice that began to resonate again in my soul. I cultivated an intimacy with God that allowed me to wait until I had peace before taking any actions.

> *Trust me, when your feet are firmly planted in faith, you may sway back and forth a little, but you are not going to be moved.*

Even after my husband told me he wanted a divorce, I waited. Communicating is my coping skill—can you tell? But during that time, I barely spoke to my husband. I didn't even send an email to my husband without complete peace. God helped me to keep my mouth shut and stay focused on Him. God began to say, "I need you to pray for this man." I thought, well, I *am* praying for him. But actually, God was telling me to remain committed to my husband and treat him as if he had done nothing wrong. Really, God? The people in my life thought I was crazy. Sometimes I felt I was crazy too. Even pastors told me I should get divorced and that I should leave him. But God had set my expectations, and I knew that if I stayed the course that I would come through this a stronger, more compassionate person.

And then, only a couple of months after my husband had left me, I was diagnosed with cancer. During that time, I was fully expecting God to bring back my hubby back and restore our relationship. I have journal entries that are scribbled with frantic, desperate prayers. I lived for years trusting and believing that God would restore our marriage. At one point, my ex-husband asked, "Why are you not divorcing me?"

The truth was that he wanted me to divorce him because he didn't want to do it. And I said, "You know what? Until God wakes me up in the middle of the night and tells me it's time to do something else, I am going to stay the course." I knew I was aligned with God, and even though I didn't understand or like what was going on, I finally had peace. Once you have tasted and experienced God's peace, you will stop at nothing to keep it. I was not about to give that up because that's what was giving me life.

Sure enough, one night God woke me up in the middle of the night and said, "It's time for a change, and you need to go talk to someone about this."

I remained obedient through all of those years, but it was hard. I could fill an empty ocean bed with the tears that were shed during that time. I survived by taking it one moment at a time. I knew that I had done every single thing in my power to allow God to do what He needed to do. It was a long process, and it was a daily choice. Most days, I didn't feel like believing in anything. I felt like laying on that floor for eight hours a day, and sometimes I did. Eventually, those eight hours became six hours. Then four hours, and then one hour, until finally, I decided that I could walk with peace, joy, and gratitude even though I was broken and hurt. I believed God had a plan for my life and that I could trust in His expectations rather than my own. I took to heart Jeremiah 29:11, which says, "'For I know the plans I have for you,' declares the LORD, 'plans to prosper you and not to harm you, plans to give you hope and a future.'"

God has a way of taking the worst circumstances and using them for our benefit. I am not saying that God wants terrible things to happen to us. I want you to take to heart that while God allows trials and conflict, chaos and suffering don't last forever. When we trust Him, He creates the opportunity for growth and greatness. When we allow Him to move, He will enable us to

> *"For I know the plans I have for you," declares the LORD, "plans to prosper you and not to harm you, plans to give you hope and a future."*

emerge victorious from even the most complicated and heart-breaking situations. God uses these situations to make Himself real to us. That difficult time put me in a place where I needed to choose God. He was my only option. I didn't have to be afraid of what might happen anymore because I was now seeking God first. The Bible instructs us to seek first the kingdom of God and His righteousness. My mantra is, "God first and then everything else."

This can be a hard idea to stand firm in, especially when you feel like the bottom has just dropped out from underneath your whole life. It feels like being thrown into a deep lake fully clothed, where you have to tread water with an enormous weight trying to pull you under. That is the moment when hope will save you. Hope is your lifeboat, and even though waiting for the storm to pass is hard, you can miraculously be at peace in the midst of it.

Hope is your lifeboat.

Has God told you to do something? Has He given you a vision, and you don't know exactly where you're going or what you're doing? This is a good thing! Don't be distracted about the uncertainty. Stay the course. God's surprises are the only ones that you can always count on to exceed your expectations. People might think you're crazy, but you'll have peace because you've cultivated an intimate relationship with God. There will be more room for joy because you will have given up the need to control every detail. You'll walk in faith, knowing that He's got you and His plans for you are real. Your circumstances may be uncertain, but that doesn't change the plan. Circumstances don't change God.

Letting go of our need to set God's expectations and instead allowing Him to set ours makes room for all kinds of crazy joy!

It seems like a good time to **stop and pray**, so I'll offer this one up for you and ME. But feel free to improvise and make it your own. This is your time to communicate with God.

God, let me rest in the eternal realm. Help me to know more clearly who you are and how much you love me. Let me leave behind what should be forgotten and seek that which you would like me to find. Let my heart be grateful for all that has already been given. Let my plans for everything be spirit molded and love-driven. Help me to strive to be as familiar with you as you are with me. Let the intimacy we share saturate my soul with patience, peace, and joy. Help me to let go of my own expectations and lean into your promises that are hidden in my heart. Let me walk boldly through the pastures of pleasure and furnaces of fire knowing that you've always got me! Amen

Make It Personal

What are your expectations of life? What are you expecting of yourself, your friends, your family and your God? How are those expectations being formed, curated, and defined?

——————————— Without judgment for yourself

I challenge you take a longish moment and get to a place where you can really be honest. Then answer this question: Who and what do you believe in? Write it down, record it, draw a doodle about it… whatever helps you get to your truth.

Now check in with yourself. How are your beliefs impacting your hope? How could life change if you really believed that God was always going to exceed your expectations?

What can you do **RIGHT NOW** to make room for more over-the-top God-sized dreams?

The Pace of Grace

"Desires shift when you are surrounded by enough space to hear the voice of God."

Let's get real for a moment about the spirit of busyness!
Life can be overwhelming, and lately it seems that every time
someone asks me how things are going, I respond with, "Busy. So
busy." I don't know about you, but busyness is a skill that I have
totally mastered! I can be on vacation, lying on a stunning beach
with no cell service, and still feel busy. It doesn't just fill my life, but
it clutters my mind and spirit as well. It is a gremlin that I am always
trying to outrun, yet also routinely returning to in times of unrest.
Busyness helps me feel in control when I am faced with uncertainty. Busyness makes me feel useful when I have slipped into the
garments of self-loathing and uselessness that seem to be my go-tos
when my spirit is exhausted. Busyness provides reasonable excuses
for why I cannot do what I know God has called me to do. For me,
extreme busyness is most often the result of displaced fear. Do you
ever find yourself trying to fill the time and space with distractions
and activities to avoid truly giving attention to what is happening
right now? Busyness allows me to stay where I am—comfortable in
grief, sadness, and self-doubt. Busyness provides the perfect opportunity for me to bury my thoughts in my marriage, my job, or
whatever current crisis that is demanding my attention.

It's hard to align yourself with what God wants when your soul is drenched in the spirit of busyness. Your prayers become all about the quick fixes that propel you from one chaotic moment to the next. These distractions prevent you from seeing even a glimpse of what God *really* wants for you.

Are you open to letting God shift your perspective away from the chaos and into the calm? Are you open to trusting God enough to ask Him, "God, please weigh my motives. You know my heart, and you know my situation. I need you to intervene here and shift me toward you because, in my own strength, I cannot do it." Are you curious about what might happen if you were to stop for a moment, relinquish some control, and learn to listen to the Spirit-driven voice that is buried deep beneath the busyness?

When my first marriage began to fall apart, I was grasping at everything that I already possessed—my marriage, my dreams, my expectations, to name just a few items. I was holding so tightly to those things that I was unable to grasp the hand of God. I didn't trust that God had everything under control. I didn't believe that He loved me or truly understood the pain I was going through. I didn't understand how He could allow my husband and our relationship to be torn away from me. Each moment that separated us felt like someone was ripping the skin off my body. I did not know who I was without this man, and I was terrified. I was fixed on holding on to everything that I had wanted for that relationship, myself, and my career. I was supposed to be a great opera singer, a great wife, and have a picture-perfect marriage. "God, don't you remember that is what I had planned for. I felt like a fraud and a failure. And then, I was diagnosed with cancer. Was this rock bottom?

I remember clearly the night that cancer introduced itself. It had been an exceptionally long year and a half, and I was tired and weary. Here I was during the most magical time of the year— autumn in New York—feeling the most alone I had ever felt. It was the last weekend in September and late into the wee hours—about 1:00 a.m. I was still not comfortable with being alone in bed, so the pillows were piled high on either side of me to mimic the warmth and comfort of a man—a husband. I had trouble sleeping, and often found myself reading my Bible late into the night. I would read and pray and cry. I would grasp on to all of the truths I had been taught as a child—"His grace is sufficient ..." "He is close to the brokenhearted ..." "Those who put their trust in Him will not be ashamed ..." Repeating these promises seemed to keep me warm in the darkest, coldest hours of hurt and despair. That night, I heard a clear voice, not distinguishable as man or woman, but a voice full of kindness and power. "Do a breast self-exam." Those are the words that were spoken. What? Even with such clarity, I was still confused.

I listened more closely, and the voice repeated itself, "Do a breast self-exam."

This was strange, but the voice, which I believe was God, was strong and direct. Immediately, I noticed the lump. My heart raced as I frantically asked myself, "How long has this been here? Am I imagining things? Can this be real?" That was the night that cancer revealed itself. Its grasp was tight and terrifying. It was there, alone in the room with me and God.

It's impossible to capture the journey of a cancer patient in the pages of a book, because when cancer chooses you, your life transforms, and the change that occurs continues for a lifetime. How you see your past, how you live in the present, and how you imagine the future are instantly altered. Your relationships are reconfigured, and the landscape of life that you were once familiar with becomes an untamed wilderness. It's like those shows *Naked and Afraid* and *Survivor*. You are dropped off in a foreign land, totally exposed, with a bunch of people you don't know, and you are expected to fight your way to the end.

There is nothing like a cancer diagnosis or any other major crisis to help shift your perspective on everything—life goals, God, relationships ... did I mention it changes everything?!

Left and abandoned by my first love, I felt less than. Repeating in my head all of the lies about myself that he had told me. I was not sexually attractive and that I was easy to lie to—Woah! That's a lot to handle on its own, but now cancer? Now, I will have scarred breasts and no hair. How will I ever win back my love? Will anyone ever find me attractive again? These questions became an ongoing torment in my life.

Pre-cancer, I had great hair! I mean *really* great hair. People always complimented me on my "crown of glory," and over time, I began to believe that it was my hair that made me beautiful, desirable, and sexy. So how do you prepare for the day that your hair begins to fall out in clumps on your pillow? The day your scalp starts to tingle and itch, and with every scratch, another bunch drops to the floor? How do you prepare for the day that you know is coming, when you need to shave it all off?

Answer: The same way you prepare for any crisis. You prepare by knowing ahead of time that difficult things are going to happen. You prepare by having an established faith and a hope that cannot be destroyed because of suffering or despair. You prepare by accepting that some things just need to be experienced. You gift yourself the grace and space to experience all the feelings while staying linked to a never-ending power source. You choose ahead of time to be kind to yourself in every moment and allow room for the crazy reactions, sadness, and sorrow to flow. Remember, the journey toward joy is paved with sorrows and grief.

At my first chemo appointment, my favorite nurse, Norma, reached out, touched my hair, and then said with conviction, "Darling, you are gonna need to cut this off." UGH.

This was when I met the incredibly talented Eugene and Adrian at the ultra-posh Rita Hazan Salon on Fifth Avenue in New York City. A friend graciously took me there to say goodbye to the lovely locks that I had been grasping. That afternoon, Eugene and Adrian skillfully cut and colored every treasured strand of hair. But more importantly, they cared for my fragile heart. This day, they were not hair stylists, but healers—comforters. They had entered into the realm of a caregiver. My soul needed a heavy dose of care, and that afternoon, God provided exactly what I needed in the form of A-list stylists in a fancy NYC salon.

My friend, who made the arrangements, held my hand for the big snip, and I held my breath. The strands were carefully brushed and pulled back into a loose ponytail before the "big snip." I can still remember the sound of the scissors slowly slicing through my thick beautiful hair. Then, a foot-long piece of hair released, and a part of me instantly withered away. There was a rush of relief and total devastation. This moment made the cancer feel real. As we all smiled through our tears, the hair was carefully placed in a bag, ready to be shipped to "Locks of Love."

Because we're friends and I told you I would always be honest, I need to confess something—I never sent the hair. I kept this hair in a bag in my dresser for many years. I could not part with it. There is something to be said for expensive shampoo because that bag of hair smelled wonderful years later! It might seem weird or even gross that I kept this hair for so long. I only told a few people because I was embarrassed—everyone thought I donated the hair, and that was a much better story than this:

She cut the hair off, stuffed it in a paper bag, and hid it in the dresser next to her bed. Sometimes, when she was feeling sad, she would pull out the hair, hold it in her hands, smell it, and be reminded of an easier time when the bliss of ignorance saturated her life...

That girl sounds a bit creepy. But that girl was me. My identity and self-worth were anchored to those strands. They represented an easier time, a less complicated season of life. They were a reminder of my youth, my health, and my beauty. Those strands were the ME that I wanted people to see—the woman that was not scarred by cancer and betrayal. Everyone told me how chic I looked. I guess they were right, but I felt like my strength had been stripped away. I was having an identity crisis. Short-haired girls were confident and fun, and I had been told that I was neither one of those things.

Later that night, after a long hot shower, I stood in front of the steamy mirror, waiting for my reflection to reveal itself. Slowly, one small glimpse at a time, my new, bare, and short-haired self was uncovered. No makeup, earrings, or hair product—just me with extremely short hair. I remembered at this moment how alone I was. It was haunting, and I was afraid of everything that was still to come. My skin was sullen from the first chemo treatment, and I began to cry softly. Silent weeping was something I had become accustomed to. It was the kind of weeping that comes from such a deep place of pain that there is no sound produced. That night, I was weak and desperately sad. Every desire and every dream had evaporated. Right then, I just wanted to survive.

A few weeks later, I found myself alone in my tiny Brooklyn apartment. I was sick from chemo, bald, and half-naked. I just needed a glass of water, and there was no one there to get it for me. I didn't have the energy to get myself out of bed. I remember being intensely angry.

A strong presence filled the room that evening. It's hard to describe it unless you've experienced it, but it was there. And I heard that voice—the kind and powerful one. "Choose me. I am here. I see you. I've got you." This was a turning point for me.

Up until this point in my life, I spent a lot of time telling God what I wanted and what I needed, but truthfully I am not sure that I really understood the difference. A broken heart really isn't the best advisor. I certainly wasn't patiently waiting for God to show me the way. I am a doer, and I feel most comfortable when my hands are full.

What do you want, and what do you need, and are you sure you understand the difference?

We all have things that we want (desires) and things that we need (necessities). The problem isn't with knowing. We have NO problem determining these things. The difficulty comes in putting the right items in each category. Distinguishing between these two things is vital when it comes to gaining clarity on what will make room for more joy in our lives, no matter what the circumstance. It is also critical to understand what is informing and motivating those wants and needs. When you are in the middle of any problematic situation or perhaps waiting for a dream to be realized, it can feel like your needs are not being met and your desires are not being recognized. I cannot tell you how many times I have shouted at, yelled at, and accosted God for not answering me or providing for me in the ways I believed my needs should be met.

"God, WHERE ARE YOU? Are you there? Why have you forsaken me? Why have you left me alone in this place of uncertainty with nowhere to go? Why have you piled suffering and hurt on top of me? Don't you see me? I need (insert your pain point here) Why won't you answer me? Why do you not love me the way you love other people?"

Maybe this one-sided conversation sounds familiar. Have you ever been exasperated with God or your circumstances? Have you ever convinced yourself that God doesn't care about what you want or need? I'd like to suggest an alternate way for all of us to look at this situation. Let's consider that perhaps what we think we want and need to feel content and provided for isn't entirely accurate.

The night before I was to undergo my first cancer-related surgery, I'd been invited to a Tuesday night prayer meeting at church. I was new in this faith community, and I didn't know many people. The plan was to introduce me to a few of the pastors so they could pray for me during that evening's service. The church was busy that evening, and I kind of got pushed aside. I entered the church, feeling desperate, invisible, and deflated. Before the service started, someone did end up praying for me at the altar. I don't remember what was said, but I do remember hearing that kind and powerful voice again, "Do not be distracted by all of the things that are going on in your life right now. Do not be distracted by what you want or by the things that have been taken away from you. Do not be distracted by this crisis or by what's about to happen. I will be with you."

After the service ended, as I sat quietly crying, the lead pastor came down off the platform, reached back to the row where I was seated, asked who I was, and then said he felt like he needed to pray for me. I know now that was God saying, "I see you, and I need you to stop clinging to everything and everyone else and start clinging to me."

You see, I had stopped dreaming or imagining that there was something more for me. I was just surviving. I wasn't thriving, I was merely enduring. I was in a deep embrace with disappointment, pain, anger, resentment, and hurt. This night marked the start of my journey toward stillness. I didn't seek out this situation. I didn't want to be still. I was most comfortable being busy and filling my hands up with anything that would mask the unbearable emptiness of feeling alone. But God knew what I needed. He knew that both my broken body and my shattered soul required a special kind of spirit-driven rest for the healing to begin. He knew that for me to thrive, the pace of my life had to be recalibrated. I had been accustomed to the rush of the hustle and the frenzy of fear. God wanted me to become acquainted with the pace of grace.

God wanted me to become acquainted with the pace of grace.

There's a pace to God's grace. The first time I heard this term was in a podcast with Sam Collier and Pastor Mike Todd from Transformation Church in Tulsa, Oklahoma. Pastor Mike said that God had given him a word for his church. God was telling him, "You need to do less so that I can do more." The pace of grace isn't exhausting. There is time built in for stillness, rest, and joy. Confidence and clarity are easy to find when you are operating at the pace of grace.

I had ended up in a place where I felt like I couldn't trust God to lead the way. I had all of these assumptions about what I thought my life was going to look like, and when things didn't turn out the way I envisioned, instead of trusting that God had a plan, I quit dreaming altogether. I was apathetic. I just wanted things to stay the same and not get any worse. Most of the time, God's plan isn't our plan. He knows better than we do what we need versus what we want. Often the first step to filling our arms up with blessings and growing through grief is choosing to let go of everything that we think we know. Do you need to let go of something? I sure did.

Amidst the chaos of cancer and separation, God brought me to the place where surrendering my need to hypothesize about what's going to happen in every situation wasn't necessary. Truthfully, I was so exhausted that I didn't even care to figure it out anymore. I didn't choose stillness. Stillness chose me. I was out of options, and surrendering to God was my last hope, even though I was still angry with Him. I wanted to trust Him and His perfect timing, but I was afraid. Thankfully, when we draw close to God, He draws close to us and wipes away the fear that is holding us back from every good and perfect thing.

When we make room for God, our pace recalibrates. Desires shift when you are surrounded by enough space to hear the voice of God. How would our lives change if we were ambitious about making space for God? How different would our dreams and desires be if we fully trusted that God was capable of doing what seemed impossible?

When we draw close to God, He draws close to us and wipes away the fear that is holding us back from every good and perfect thing.

"God can do anything, you know—far more than you could ever imagine or guess or request in your wildest dreams! He does it not by pushing us around but by working within us, his Spirit deeply and gently within us."

Ephesians 3:20-21 (MSG)

God wants to exceed your expectations and do things that are above and beyond anything you can imagine. If this is true, why do we feel the need to hold tightly to the expectations and desires we have set for ourselves? Let's be clear; I am not saying that you shouldn't make plans or have goals. I don't think I could survive without the comfort of a well-thought-out plan or an expertly organized itinerary.

Goals are essential, and when our desires and dreams are being formed by God, and we are walking through life at the pace of grace they are more likely to be aligned with what we actually need. God will use our skill sets and gifts in ways that we can't imagine, but we won't have to do all the heavy lifting. We don't have to try and make it all happen on our own. When you're embedded in a crisis, you have the freedom to relinquish it all to God and say, "God, what do you need me to do? And when do I just need to rest and let you work?"

Can you imagine choosing to believe that God will use everything for your good? Imagine believing that even in the worst of circumstances, your needs will be met and there will still be room for joy.

Be aware that once you are aligned with God, there may be times that the excitement of dreams forming and doors cracking open will tempt you to get in the fast lane and bypass God. It's not that you want to move ahead without God, but you see the answered prayers, and you're so motivated that you rush forward without taking the time to be still and make sure you stay in alignment with God. Remember, you don't need to set the pace.

Let God do that. Stay ambitious about experiencing His love and resting in the place of peace so that He can prepare you to take action. Practice getting familiar with that still small voice that resonates deep within your soul. God wants you to dream big, walk in a place of hope, and remember that your desires and needs are all in His view.

He wants to captivate your thoughts so your faith will be activated. And then He wants you to move forward with boldness. You get to choose if you're going to try to do things on your own, make your own plans, and ask God for His blessing after the fact or trust Him and believe that He's going to exceed your expectations from the beginning. You might not see it or feel it at the moment, but believing that God has something great in store for you is guaranteed to bring more joy into your life. This mindset will also spill out and increase the joy quotients of each person you come in contact with. Who doesn't like to be around a joyful dreamer?

Let me help reset your expectations: You will experience moments when you don't understand why your desires are not coming to pass, and you may have to wrestle with God!

Don't be afraid to lock yourself alone in a room with God and say, "God, I want to get to know you as well as you know me. You already know what's going on in my heart, and I don't like it. I don't like this situation. I have these desires, but it seems like you're passing me by. Still, I'm going to place my hope in you, and I'm asking you to exceed my expectations. And I commit that when you give me direction, I'm going to follow through even if it's hard."

We have already determined that to get real about joy, you need to get real about suffering and God. But to get real about God, you need to get real *with* God. You have to be upfront and totally transparent with everything that you want, and I mean everything! Even the stuff that you feel uncomfortable acknowledging. It's okay, God can handle it. The truth is, he already knows. He is just waiting for you to be honest with Him (and yourself). Get it all out and then watch God trim and transform that list into something you couldn't have imagined.

After my first husband left, I prayed and prayed that he would return. Then he did, and almost instantly, I reverted to allowing my relationship with him to be my source of self-confidence, self-esteem, and self-love. I was distracted by the blessing. Once again, I started compartmentalizing God and thinking about my future without considering God's plan or purpose.

I didn't even know what was happening. I was so excited after all those years of praying for my husband to come back that I stopped seeking the stillness of God. The next thing I know, my anxiety was high, things weren't going well, and I realized I was no longer aligned with God's pace but instead right back to struggling through the frenzy of fear.

You see, it's a process. I don't want to make it seem like it's easy, because it isn't. I have an entrepreneurial spirit, and there are times when that makes life more challenging because I have lots of ideas and dreams for myself and for everyone around me. I'm an expert planner and often forget that to navigate this complicated life, I still need to be disciplined about how I'm caring for my soul. I need to have the courage to be obedient to that still small voice that resonates inside.

God knows what you want and what you need. Trust Him to exceed your expectations. Sure, you can go about your business, stumbling along and doing things your way. God will continue to use you because there's work to be done. But if you desire to embrace all that He has for you, experience joy, and a peace that passes all understanding, you must choose to align yourself with God regardless of what is going on in your life. Are you willing to do that? It will take courage and boldness, but what you'll get in return will be amazing.

God knows that you are bursting with anticipation for the next season to begin. Be reminded that God is the ultimate creator and you have been made in His image. So be encouraged. Keep dreaming and walking in hope. Your visions, wants, and needs are in His view. Let your faith be activated so your thoughts are captivated by God's love and guidance. And then, with boldness— ask, seek, and knock, knowing by faith that good things are on the horizon.

"Keep on asking, and you will receive what you ask for. Keep on seeking, and you will find. Keep on knocking, and the door will be opened to you."
Matthew 7:7 (NLT)

Make It Personal

Honestly, what do you want? What are the desires that are hidden deeply in your soul?

Without judgment for yourself I challenge you to write them all down or say them out loud in front of a mirror!

Now check in with yourself. How are you feeling now? What's your joy quotient today? Are you satisfied? Is there room for more joy and more peace?

What can you do **RIGHT NOW** to let go, align yourself with God, and make room to experience all that He has in store for you?

Every Moment is a Destination

"And we know that God causes everything to work together for the good of those who love God and are called according to his purpose for them."
Romans 8:28 (NLT)

Do you have something that brings you comfort when things are hard? For me, Romans 8:28 is one of my favorite Bible verses. It brought me great comfort during the many times in my life when I could not make sense of anything; when circumstances appeared to be hopeless, and it seemed impossible for anything good to emerge from the pain I was enduring. I clung to the truth that is embedded in this verse when I had nothing else to cling to, when everything and everyone that I'd hoped would bring me happiness and joy seemed to have failed.

My life is a living testimony of this verse's exact sentiment. If my ex-husband had not left me for the second time, then I would have never ended up at the church where God would reignite my love of singing and lead me to my soulmate, Mr. Walker. I also probably wouldn't be writing this book. God actually did transform my messed up circumstances into something beautiful.

But as much as I like this Bible verse, sometimes I don't like embracing the "His purpose" portion. Because the truth is that often God's purpose and our mission collide. It can feel like we are on opposite teams. How can suffering, loss, and hurt be a part of the purpose for our lives? This is as hard a concept to understand as the saying, "Everything happens for a reason." Really? Everything? I am pretty sure that using this statement to comfort yourself or someone else who is knee-deep in devastation won't prove to be helpful. The last thing I wanted to hear when surrounded by the deafening silence of miscarriage was that everything happens for a reason or God was going to use this for my good. So how can God's higher purpose be something that we discover and step into without becoming bitter, resentful, and apathetic? How can every moment be savored and fully experienced? How can we squeeze every ounce of joy and gratitude out of even the most desperate of times?

The first step is to accept that we will never completely understand everything, and that's okay. We were not intended to fully understand how God can transform problems into a purpose. Yet, by faith, it is something that we can embrace. It's complicated—just like everything else in life! God's purpose for us and everyone else is defined by details and elements that are too complex to grasp because He sees all things, hears all things, and knows all things. Sometimes we spend so much time trying to understand God's plans and purpose that we forget to experience God right here and right now. It's within the experience that we become equipped to step into the purpose of each and every moment.

Sometimes we spend so much time trying to understand God's plans and purpose that we forget to experience God right here and right now.

There are many memories from my first marriage and its failing that continue to hold considerable space in my memory bank. This can, at times, evoke experiences of guilt because I feel disloyal to Mr. Walker by mingling with these old instincts. But it's important to mention because divorce, separation, and breakups are regular parts of life. No one seems to care if it is your first, second, or third marriage. Total monogamy and the quest for purity have become antiquated concepts. I hold no judgment against anyone regarding their personal relationship choices. But I can tell you from experience that when you give yourself over to physical and spiritual intimacy, a bond is created; it's sacred, strong, and supernatural. When this bond that you have nurtured and cultivated is severed, there are repercussions.

There are no clean cuts in a divorce, even when it's the right option. By the time my divorce was finalized, I was at peace. I knew that God had a plan, yet I still didn't understand the "why" behind this experience. I had difficulty reconciling the purpose of the thousands of prayers I'd offered up for a man whom I was no longer linked to. To this day, there are both happy and horrible memories from that relationship which are still vivid in my mind and heart. I will probably never escape them, and perhaps that's the point. The intensity of these memories and the conflicted feelings of love and anger that I still hold for my ex-husband are a constant reminder of how important it is to nurture the love that is right in front of me.

They remind me to be present. People often ask me if I regret the pain of that first marriage, or if I would go back and do it again if I could warn myself. The answer is a very emphatic NO!

Listen, the best thing that ever happened to my current marriage was my first marriage! For real, though. I am a kinder, more gracious, and less self-righteous partner because of my painful past relationship. And having the ability to recall with clarity how painful the breaking of that bond was is vital. It helps me to value what I have and work extra hard to be sure that I never have to experience anything like that again.

But there is a difference in seeing the value embedded in past experiences and deciding to sit down and take a long soak in them! Dwelling in the past makes it impossible to experience the purpose of the present. Cancer, crises, and disappointments have taught me that life isn't lived in months

> *Dwelling in the past makes it impossible to experience the purpose of the present.*

or years, it is lived moment by moment. Each moment is a destination and allowing yourself to be present, and experience joy are the keys to living a more peaceful and abundant life. This makes sense to most people, in theory, but saying it doesn't make it possible if you don't know how to attain it. How do you stop and smell the roses if the world around you seems to reek of pain and suffering? How can you be present and choose gratitude, peace, and joy when everything is going wrong? How is that possible?

Life isn't lived in months or years, it is lived moment by moment.

Growing up in the church, I was constantly surrounded by phrases like "You just gotta have faith," or "God is good," or "Just give it to God." and while those statements are true, there's much more to the process of enduring a crisis than merely reciting a few words. I have struggled with finding peace and joy amidst the worst circumstances, and I have been frustrated when people attack with their faith-filled, uber-excited encouragement. You know what I am talking about! It's that aggressive encouragement that beats you into submission and forces you to say you are okay when you honestly are not. You end up cowering in the corner, shaking in the fetal position, and repeating over and over, "God is good," even though you don't believe that. Of course, speaking encouragement in love is a positive thing, but it's not helpful if you can't also acknowledge that life straight up sucks sometimes. It doesn't matter who you are or how much faith you have, it's not easy to find purpose and peace in the middle of the storm. Remember what I said at the beginning of this book? The reason why I talk about joy so much and take on the title "joy seeker" is because it's a constant journey for me. Life is tough, and joy seems to instantly evaporate at times, especially when we cannot figure out the purpose of the pain and disappointment.

This is why I need God. And when I say God, I mean Jesus too. The joy of the Lord is my strength. Other writers, speakers, and professional motivators will offer flashier, more inspirational bite-sized tips on how to navigate a crisis and be fully present than I will. But as earlier discussed, I am only an expert at my own crises, and I am not going to pretend to be an expert at yours. Sure, I have enough life experiences that I too could curate a book full of inspirational tips and suggestions that may or may not get you closer to your happy place, but in my opinion, that wouldn't be offering you my best. The most helpful thing I can do is tell you what's worked for me and what I know to be true. My hope is that you will take this information and start to see your own life differently, that you will begin to see the possibility where you once only saw pain. I pray that you will become comfortable with the prospect of suffering because you are confident that amidst the most troubling times, there are opportunities for growth and the assurance of joy.

I am alive today because of the faith and hope that I continue to place in the almighty God. This is the first and foremost step in embracing joy and stepping into the destination of each moment. I don't think you can do it on your own; I know that I cannot.

God's guidance is trustworthy and reliable and doesn't require a manufactured or romanticized narrative. It's essential to be realistic about the fact that there is nothing neat and tidy about this journey toward a more purposeful life, a life that is readily receptive to unlimited servings of gratitude, peace, and joy. The best way for you to make room for more joy is to get to know God—because God is an expert at *everyone's* crisis, and He will prepare you to tackle each problem that comes your way. This preparation is a gift and it's part of your purpose. knowing this allows you the opportunity to be in the moment and always totally present.

> *God is an expert at everyone's crisis, and He will prepare you to tackle each problem that comes your way.*

Enduring multiple rounds of chemotherapy is the perfect way to shift your perspective on a variety of topics. Chemo, for me, was hard. I mean painstakingly hard. It was a combination of total physical, spiritual, and emotional depletion. I began treatment as a woman in the middle of an emotional betrayal by the person closest to me, and cancer intensified that betrayal; even my own body was trying to extinguish me. Some days, the thought of getting from the bed to the bathroom, then to the fridge and back to bed felt like the Tour de France. It was exhausting.

Then one morning, about four days after a treatment cycle, I awakened and the chemo fog that I was familiar with started to dissipate. For a brief moment, I felt a wave of peace and gratitude. The sun was shining through my window, my coffee tasted extra delicious, and there was a residue of satisfaction on the toast that I routinely forced myself to choke down. That moment, I remember thinking, "This here is a destination; this very moment is an opportunity for something." **Every moment is gifted with the possibility of joy, but to experience it, you will have to make a conscious effort to pause, choose gratitude, and look in the direction of hope. Peace and joy's availability isn't impacted by the severity of your circumstances but instead your willingness to acknowledge their presence and invite them to be a part of your journey.**

Before cancer, I probably wouldn't have noticed the food or coffee or the sun streaming through my window because they were just everyday things, a few of the many things that I took for granted. But that day, I truly experienced this moment, and as a result, I *was* joy; I embodied it, embraced it, and experienced it. My gratitude for small, simple pleasures made room at the table of pain for a heaping serving of joy. The circumstances were still dire. I'd still been betrayed by my husband and my cancer wasn't gone, but at that moment, my burdens were lifted, and life felt less weighty. I became the light in the middle of my own dark tunnel. I realized that it was possible to have those moments and access joy on my own terms. It also gave me permission to have times that were the opposite, days and moments when I couldn't get out of bed or the food didn't taste good and I couldn't recognize the warmth of the sun coming through my window. I experienced many days when the pain overshadowed everything else. But hope and gratitude helped me. The defining factor that kept me reaching was remembering that there were more good days on the horizon. I wasn't in control of every ache or pain, but I was in control of my ability to be grateful, which meant I was also in control of my joy. I could increase my joy quotient as needed.

For every utterly crappy day, I felt more grateful for the good ones. I began appreciating the small details of each moment. The pain I was experiencing made me more susceptible to gratitude because I was looking more closely at each given moment as an opportunity for something, anything beyond just purposeless pain. The more grateful I was, the more things I found to be thankful for.

Gratitude turned out to be the miracle drug that I'd been searching for. I was living life moment to moment, each one a destination full of possibility. As it turns out, this attitude of gratitude was contagious. I needed the combination of the pain and the joy to create the impact that God had planned.

Opportunities presented themselves to share my pain with others who were also suffering, but I was also able to share my joy. Each interaction became a destination—whether it was the cashier at the drug store or the nurse taking my blood. I began to see that living for the *end* of the cancer wasn't the goal anymore. That wasn't going to help me impact others each day—amidst my trial. Waiting idly for the end of the crisis wasn't going to help me operate in the purpose that God had for that season of my life. God wanted to use me right then! In the middle of the mess, God was building my character, clarifying my purpose, and using my pain.

Moment by moment, He was shaping me and using me to impact the lives of other people. When you allow God to shift your perspective and you acknowledge that He has a purpose for every single moment that He has gifted you, then you will see opportunities that you may have never seen before.

To thrive through suffering, I have to stay focused on what I know. I grasp on to the smallest piece of truth and let God take care of the rest. You can do this too! When you move your focus to the little things and let God focus on the big stuff, you can take ownership of every moment and trust that God is taking care of everything else!

People ask me, "What did you do when you got cancer or when you realized that having biological children might be impossible? How did you function after making a choice to have a surgery that would force menopause to save your life?" These are hard questions, and when you are on the other side of your own sufferings, people will want to know the magic answer as to how you survived. They will assume that because you have been through so much that you must know all the answers. The truth is, I don't have any more answers than you have. You can only do what you know, even if it is something as simple as praying. There were days when that was all I could do. God will not give you more than you can handle (with His help, of course), so live in the moment, knowing that God is in there with you. You don't have to know what to do next because God is taking care of *all your* tomorrows.

The Gift of Gratitude

You can choose to be grateful and walk with an attitude of gratitude. That doesn't mean you have to be thankful *for* every circumstance, but you can be grateful *in* every circumstance. Each moment of your life has a purpose. Look for and live that purpose one moment at a time. As you open yourself up to this, you won't have to conjure up joy. Joy will come.

Each moment of your life has a purpose. Look for and live that purpose one moment at a time.

This is exactly what I had to learn to do. I had to open myself up to whatever it was that God wanted to do in each moment. I could either be curious about how God wanted to use my pain for good, or I could be close-minded, miserable. Think about it: Have you ever met a close-minded person who is full of peace and joy?

None of us know how many days we have left on this earth. It could be many or it could be few. Today might be it. Let's reframe our idea of purpose and start looking at every moment as purpose—full. We all desire to have an impact somewhere, to reach the masses or have a more significant influence in our work or with our passions. We plan ways to reach more followers and cast a wider net—yet often by looking so far into the future, we miss the opportunities of today. The notion that we must hustle toward some ethereal, undefined "purpose" can be debilitating and depressing. It will steal your peace and make gratitude virtually impossible. And there is no room for joy at the party if gratitude isn't already present.

Are you wondering when God will promote you or when you will see the dream come to pass? Are you tormented by the thoughts that God has forgotten you and doesn't have a purpose for you? Please resist the urge to sit down and wallow in the pools of self-pity, close-mindedness, and hopelessness. Take a breath and find something, anything to be grateful for. Be content, trusting that God does have a plan that is taking into consideration everything. His timing always proves to be perfect.

"So be content with who you are, and don't put on airs. God's strong hand is on you; he'll promote you at the RIGHT time. Live carefree before God; he is MOST careful with you."
1 Peter 5:6-7 (MSG, emphasis added)

So today, do what you know to do!

Give yourself over to the work that is in front of you. Look for opportunities to be grateful, show kindness, and spread joy. Believe that even the smallest, most insignificant tasks can have an eternal impact when they are done with great love and intention.

Tomorrow is not promised. But today is HERE! Be curious about how God might want to use you in whatever you may be going through. Be on the lookout for the pockets of purpose contained in each moment. That's all you need to focus on because God is taking care of the larger picture. **Each moment is a destination, and you only have to get to one at a time.**

How easy is it for you to "let go and let God?" What steals your focus and blocks your ability to live "in the moment?"

——————————— Without judgment for yourself

I challenge you to pause → choose gratitude → and then look in the direction of hope. Just do it! Please. Don't judge it or think about it too much.

Now check in with yourself. How does it feel to pause? Was it easy, or did you find it difficult? How did you decide to choose gratitude? When you looked in the direction of hope, where were you looking?

What can you do **RIGHT NOW** to make room for gratitude and see the purpose (and the joy) in every moment?

Let's Get Real about Fear

Despite the more than thirty-five years since it happened, I can still remember the pain and fear that I experienced when a jagged piece of metal sliced through my skin as I was running around outside in my backyard. I am sure that my hands were dirty from climbing trees, so there were plenty of opportunities for a significant infection to settle into the wound. My mom wasn't home, but my dad was outside next to our tiny red and white sailboat with a young woman who had stopped by to inquire about purchasing it. As soon as my skin was pierced, and my eyes saw the blood, my strong vocal cords took over.

I let out a scream that surely scared the neighbors. My dad instantly turned and came running, the woman trailing close behind. As you can imagine, I was inconsolable, screaming like crazy, tear-stained, and covered in blood. Not only was I completely disoriented, but my dad was too. I remember him hugging me and trying to talk to me, but I think we were both in shock. Maybe it is just because women seem to be better at handling crises with kids, but this young woman took over. I don't know if she was a nurse or simply extremely good at managing bad situations. But the next thing I remember is sitting at our tiny kitchen table with this lovely woman cleaning my wound, applying antibiotic ointment, and offering up that motherly comfort that seems to make everything heal more quickly. I felt safe, comforted, and cared for. Her encouragement was akin to an extra-strong pain reliever. Her take-charge attitude not only got me all cleaned up, but it put both my dad and me at ease. By the time she left, I was feeling like myself and eager to go climb another tree. I don't have any other memories of that incident. I don't remember feeling significant prolonged pain or any recurrent infections. Even though this incident was scary, it wasn't that severe. I was a young kid with a healthy immune system that could easily fight off a hint of infection with just a small about of care and treatment. Sure, I have a small scar, but I actually like the scar. It reminds me of that lovely woman. It reminds me of my father's hugs, which I never truly appreciated and of that little family sailboat, which was the vessel of beautiful childhood memories.

Do you remember getting hurt as a kid?

Getting the kind of scratch that ends up infected and leaves behind a scar that will help you to remember that moment forever. Most small wounds usually only require some disinfectant, and a little Neosporin to get the healing started. Sure they might leave a scar, but the repercussions are not life-altering.

Sometimes infections are isolated and eradicated quickly; other occurrences are more severe, like when I had a bilateral mastectomy. The radiation treatments that I underwent before this surgery made my skin fragile and susceptible to infection. This complicated the healing process after surgery. Seasons with pain and suffering are like those more severe occurrences. They require more than just a little dab of antibiotic ointment to get us through without causing additional complications and increased misery. When we are vulnerable because of a season of suffering, we are more susceptible to the infections of fear and doubt. We need an extra dose of something to keep us from experiencing prolonged pain. Faith is necessary to strengthen our spiritual immune system and lessen the possibility of future attacks. Trials prove to be harder when you try to fight the burdens all alone. God is gracious and will provide practical support when necessary—just like the woman who stepped in to patch up my shoulder. But ultimately, God wants us to trust Him for ourselves. He wants to build your spiritual immune system so you can ward off the attacks of fear, doubt, and discouragement when obstacles appear in your life. What is your first response to fear?

When you are susceptible to fear and doubt, it can feel impossible to trust God. You can feel hopeless. The first step to strengthening your spiritual immune system is to acknowledge how you're feeling. This is where healing begins. If you don't recognize your real feelings, then you end up carrying the weight of them with you. They become like a dormant infection just waiting to reemerge.

When I was going through chemotherapy, one of my bimonthly treatments was a fuchsia-colored chemo drug that they would deliver to my bedside in a bag marked with a bright tag labeled "TOXIC." This lifesaving, yet toxic, fluid was slowly and carefully injected directly into a vein on my wrist. It was needed to kill the lingering cancer cells that were floating around in my body. When administered too quickly, this liquid tears through the veins, damages the tissue, and usually causes an infection. One day, that exact thing happened to me. I immediately knew something was wrong. Suddenly my arm felt icy cold and extremely hot all at the same time. Within minutes my wrist swelled up, turned red, and it felt like someone had dropped a brick on it. I had what they call an IV infiltration, and now my arm was infected. The treatment plan was to administer a standard dose of antibiotics. Each time I received this dosage, the infection appeared to clear up. But it wasn't truly gone. I just didn't notice that it was still there. As soon as I would go back for chemo and my immune system dipped, the pain and swelling returned. Eventually, I was sent to a specialist who understood that particular kind of infection. He gave me an extra portion of antibiotics to heal the root of the infection so that it would not return.

The same concept applies to life when you see God as that specialist, only this time, the infection is fear. If you do not get to the root cause of your fear and of your doubt, they will never completely heal. There will always be opportunities to be fearful and doubtful. Still, when you allow God to strengthen your spiritual immune system the same way the specialist strengthened my physical immune system, you can ward off fear and doubt as they come. When you don't take the time to acknowledge the fear, you end up avoiding it. The uncertainty burrows down into the depths of your soul, allowing it to stay dormant until the next wave of crisis comes at you, and all of a sudden it erupts again. Not only are you bombarded by the present crisis, but the remnants of your past fears also contribute to the growing contamination.

Being honest with yourself and God about all that you are feeling and experiencing makes it easier to let these unhelpful feelings go without indulging them. Letting go doesn't invalidate what you went through but replaces the emotions with something that isn't based solely on your feelings or circumstances: the knowledge and the belief that God's got you and He cares for you and has something special for you. When your broken and discouraged self takes a long, restful soak in the things of God, you are better equipped to choose hope and fight off fear.

Practically speaking, this can be extremely hard. It takes courage, tenacity, and boldness. Choosing hope is not a weak posture. Too many times in my life, I've lived in fear waiting for the other shoe to drop. For years, fear was securely fastened to whatever choice I made. What would happen if I stepped out in faith, if I started to dream again or love again? Fear paralyzed me. Instead of stepping out, I tried to keep myself in a safe zone and not do too much. I stayed timid and trapped in this space, my self-appointed protective bubble. I've come a long way in my faith journey; I still struggle. It's a constant battle. Every day, I must choose to say, "Today I will believe that I am who God says I am, and He is who He says He is. He will use my suffering to help others, and He will turn my mourning into joy." Only after loosening my grip on fear am I able to step into the abundance that God has for me. Stepping out in faith requires a healthy spiritual posture, the same way Joshua from the Old Testament had to step into the waters of the Jordan before it parted. Sometimes you have to step out in faith when the path to success has not yet been revealed. You simply have to grab on to God's hand and jump.

Meeting Mr. Walker was one of the most frustrating, jarring, and fear-filled moments in my life. He didn't swoop in and sweep me off my feet like my first husband, and it wasn't love at first sight. There were no butterflies or daydreaming about true love and a life full of joy. There was pain, confusion, apprehension, and skepticism. I met him when the wounds from the past rejections were not yet healed, and I was still susceptible to infections of fear and doubt.

Sorry to burst your bubble, but true love stories aren't often curated and orchestrated by a skilled Hollywood director and producer. They are not void of the burdens and baggage that the wounded souls of this world are clothed in. True love stories are messy and complicated. There are struggles and suffering attached to love that is birthed out of the two wounded people coming together. True love is established after and during the fight. There is a battle for true love, and both parties have to be committed to fighting on the same team for the same purpose.

I first met Lenny in the bookstore at our church. He was working the register and recognized me as a new person in the choir. He flashed his beautiful smile, asked my name, and introduced himself, "Hi, my name is Lenny—like Lenny Kravitz!"

For the last three years, I had worked hard at keeping a low profile when it came to meeting men. I avoided eye contact and made an effort to ignore any hint of a friendly advance. This was a skill that I had painstakingly developed over the years. I was good at isolating myself from any unwanted interest. You see, I was exhausted from my own circumstances. I was sick of playing the role of "the woman scorned" and didn't want to explain one more time that I was still married to a man who wanted nothing to do with me.

I didn't trust men—any men—and I was just starting to trust Jesus again. Yet for some reason, on that day I accepted this olive branch because it was benign. I couldn't sense an underlying motive beneath Lenny's pearly whites, so I smiled back, introduced myself, and went on my way.

I only remember seeing Lenny one other time that year. He brushed passed me in the sanctuary once and smiled. I remembered that smile and called out, "Hey Lenny, Lenny Kravitz!" That was it. No other interaction.

During this year, God and I had regularly scheduled wrestling matches regarding His plan for my life. I felt like Jacob in Genesis. I was so confused about what was next. At this point, I had conquered cancer during one of the most painful times of rejection I would ever face, and I desperately wanted God to do something new. For more than three years, I waited and prayed for my husband to return to his faith and to his wife I spent my free time visiting with deacons and women in need. I worked hard at a job that demanded my attention, commitment, and care. I have always been a helper, and once I was finally in remission, I focused on that skill. I thought, "If I could help everyone around me, then I will be loved and accepted. If I don't ask for too much, I might be cherished and taken care of." I kept my head down and tiptoed through life, hoping that I might just avoid another trauma.

I saw God working in other people's lives. Healings happened, love blossomed, babies were born, and careers formed, all while I was standing quietly with my face pushed up against the proverbial storefront window, hoping that someday I would get invited into the shiny place that existed on the other side. I didn't have the confidence to simply open the door and walk into this joyful place. I assumed the door was locked and that I had to wait for someone to invite me.

This was a cold and lonely existence. My soul had absorbed a considerable amount of rejection and sadness over the years, and there didn't seem to be room to soak up anything else. Sure, I knew God, and I had a deep relationship with Him. He had been my companion through many lonely nights. The little seed-sized faith that I carried around kept me sane. It prevented me from giving in to the feelings of depression and the thoughts of suicide, and it allowed me to find the small pocket of peace that was woven into each circumstance. This speck of faith was my lifeline, and because of it, I was continuing to survive. But was I thriving? Did I believe that God could and would exceed my expectations? Did I trust that God was going to use all things for my good? Did I think that I was welcome in that place that existed on the other side of the window, where all of the happy shiny people were? No. Deep down, I embraced the idea that at any moment, I might be tossed aside and discarded for something new.

Have you ever felt or thought of yourself as disposable? Let me tell you, when you see yourself as disposable, others see you this way too. They may not admit it or they might not even realize it, but somehow this happens. We teach people how to treat us, and I had become an expert at allowing others to define my value.

It took all of my energy to get dressed every Sunday and show up for church. I had never wanted to be in the choir. Truthfully, I wanted to do anything BUT be in the choir. I was totally done with singing. I had given my heart and soul over to the nurturing of this gift, and instead of experiencing success, I was burdened with rejection, debilitating performance anxiety, and pure anger toward God. What do you do when you feel like you have been given something to bless the world, and then it just never works out to use it? Why would God give me such a gift if He was going to let me fail so miserably? The breaking point came when my first husband revealed to me that he resented me for not being more of a success. *GUT PUNCH* I always say that it is more romantic to be married to an aspiring artist than a struggling artist. At the moment, this was devastating to me and to who I saw myself as. Now, when I reflect on this period, I can see how my then-husband was exhausted. I am sure that he also wondered why God had not opened the doors for my success in the way that everyone had told us would happen. Everyone said that I was going to be the next great dramatic coloratura—I had chords of steel and a voice that could pierce through even the largest orchestra. Why then had God allowed the rejections to pile up? Why did every door I encountered seem to be jammed shut and double bolted? This was a struggle for us. Unfortunately for us and for our marriage, our connection and faith were not strong enough to move us to fight together. I don't excuse his bad behavior and the sometimes-borderline abusive language he used with me, but I can understand now that he also was broken. He was searching for his own pocket of peace, and when he couldn't find it in me, he took what the world presented to him instead.

Despite waking up every single day and going to church, I was not about being in the choir! I had given up singing! I remember the day I decided to quit singing. I told the few students I had left that I would not be teaching anymore and made a plan to finish my last performance of *Cosi fan tutte* with a small group at the New York City Public Library. I dropped out of the next role I was scheduled to play and told God that I would no longer be singing. Yes, you heard me correctly—I TOLD God. Please if there is one thing that you take from this book, consider this—if you find yourself at a crossroads and you decide to tell God how it's gonna be, be assured that it is NOT going to be that way! My friend Sarah says that God is not intimidated by our fear. I will take that a step further and say that He is also not intimidated by our anger or our stubbornness. Go ahead; tell God about Himself (I still do it all the time) and then trust that He hasn't changed.

God is not intimidated by our fear.

So here I was at this big church with a great choir, and instead of jumping at the chance to join, I did everything in my power to avoid it. When people would ask what I did, who I was, and where I came from, I told them everything BUT the singing part. I may have worked my way back to a better relationship with God, but I was still so angry and hurt. I felt like God had betrayed me, just like every other man in my life. I believed the lies that I systematically recited to myself in moments of fear and doubt—You are not worthy. You will always be on the outside. You are disposable. Your desires don't matter. That was some loud self-talk! But no matter how hard I tried to drown out the real voice of God, I couldn't. I was no match for the powerful voice that pierces through the darkness of doubt and shines a light into spaces that are occupied by fear. God has ways of dragging us into the light even when we are kicking and screaming!

God has ways of dragging us into the light even when we are kicking and screaming!

One fall evening, I found myself at a karaoke bar with a few friends. It was one of those places where you get your own room, a few mics, and can sing for hours. I was not interested in this at all. I didn't want to sing—EVER. But somehow that night, I found myself belting out a few Sarah McLachlan tunes with a dear friend. I was petrified. Later that evening, one of the people we were with mentioned that I should join the choir. I glared back at this guy and let him know that I was not interested. I took it a step further by telling him that if he told anyone that I had a background in singing,

I would never speak to him again. At first, he thought I was joking, but my icy stare and unamused tone convinced him otherwise.

It was only a few weeks later that I ran into him after a prayer service. He was chasing after me in a very annoying and slightly aggressive manner. He blurted out, "Vanessa, I know you don't want to sing, and I know that you said if I ever talked about this again that you would unfriend me, but God is telling me that you should join the choir." I responded curtly, "Fine. I will meet with your aunt, but just know this is not the place for me." Oh, did I forget to mention that this guy was the nephew of the choir director? (I am rolling my eyes right now). Yes, you've got it—after not singing for over a year, I ended up in a small karaoke room with the nephew of the choir director. God always knows what He is doing.

Well, every meeting that was set up for me to sit down with the director got canceled. And each time, I reminded my friend that I wasn't meant to sing anymore. And then one evening as I was strolling into a prayer meeting, someone called my name. "Vanessa? You are Vanessa, right?—Carol (the choir director) wants to see you." I was trapped. Totally trapped.

I entered her office with trepidation and a firm plan to let this woman know that I was not interested in singing. She asked me about my life, and I eagerly told her about cancer, separation, and everything BUT the music. She then asked if I would sing something for her. My heart began to pound, and even before I could answer, she was sitting at the piano playing the intro to "Amazing Grace." The next thing I know, my mouth was open, and the sound was pouring out. When it was all over, the choir director questioned: "It sounds like you have some training?" This was the moment of truth. I could lie in a house of God or just give in to whatever He was doing. I responded, "Yes." Next, she asked me why I wanted to be in the choir. And I confidently let her know that I didn't want to be in the choir, but if she thought I should be, I would join. Her response: "Great, I will see you tomorrow night at practice."

Every day when I arrived for the choir, I started sweating and tears welled up. Each time I stepped onto the risers was an act of obedience. Earlier that year, I had committed to serving in a ministry and told God (yes, I told God again) that I would walk through whatever door He opened. So here I was doing the very thing that I told God I would never do again. My advice: NEVER tell God what you intend to do if it even remotely feels like it is against His will. He will prove you wrong.

Now you might be wondering what this has to do with Lenny. Remember our first meeting? He was also in the choir. That first year in the choir was a difficult one. I was in a life-threatening battle with doubt, and the fear factor was notably high. I routinely found myself in situations that forced me to step out in faith. I didn't want to sing, and I didn't want to be noticed. But God found ways of pushing me out of the timid, fearful place that had me trapped. The first time I ever sang with the worship team was because someone didn't show up, and the keyboard player saw me sitting in the second row of the congregation. I don't think he even knew my name. He leaned over the partition that separated the band from the audience, tapped my shoulder, and handed me a microphone. He said, "I need you to go up on stage and sing." I thought I was going to pass out. Thank God I still had that mustard seed-sized faith. It was certainly getting a workout!

When you operate with faith in uncomfortable places, you allow God an opportunity to show His strength, move through you, and magnify your impact! It also takes the pressure off because you are reminded that it's not by your might or your power that you do anything, but by the strength of God's Spirit.

It is incredible how God decided to use one of the most exposing and painful parts of my life—singing—as an instrument of healing. He used each fearful moment as an opportunity to show me His strength and remind me of my own worth. This was the preparation that I would need to love again.

That year, I wrote out a few requests for God:

1. Please release me from my current marriage and free me both financially and spiritually from my husband.
2. Please heal my broken heart so that I am ready and able to love again—soon.
3. Never make me date again.

I filed that journal entry away, and when the time was right, Lenny came back into view. I didn't know the time was right, and at first, I didn't want anything to do with a love interest. But God knew what I needed. God knew what was around the corner, and He had the perfect partner already chosen for me.

As I said before, there was no love at first sight for Lenny and me. Actually neither one of us was honestly that happy about the first meal we shared together. Remember my new friend Ebony? Well, she had invited me out for brunch because I had recently told her that I needed to get out more. I had become too comfortable living a hermit's existence and needed some practice socializing. She decided to also invite her friend Lenny. They had been friends for a long time, and Lenny treasured his moments alone with Ebony. They could eat whatever they wanted and talk like old friends do—you know what I mean! So when she showed up with me, he was less than excited. If you have ever walked into a situation you wish you hadn't, I understand. Luckily for me, God knew what He was doing. He was slowly healing my wounds from the inside out, so that I would be prepared to love again. This story was just beginning!

Finding My Voice

Have you ever lost your voice, or let someone steal it? Have the external voices in your life ever drowned out the truth and amplified the lies? Have these lies kept you paralyzed in a place of fear?

I've always struggled with fear; it is my recurring illness. With chronic diseases, you need a treatment plan. Just like a diabetic has a treatment plan to control their disease or like I had a treatment plan for cancer, you can have a treatment plan for your fear. When you land in the middle of a major crisis, you will need frequent checkups. You might even need a few hospital stays and extra-strong doses of love, encouragement, and prayer to get you through. With God on your side, you have access to the greatest healer ever! But don't forget that even when you are feeling better, you still need an expert to check in with to be sure there are not any signs of a recurrence. This is the preventative medicine which increases your awareness and strengthens your immune system so that you are prepared when the next wave of crisis comes your way. You have to frequently be reminded of the truth of who God is and who He says you are, not only during the difficult times, but in the good times too. Having faith in God is something that must be maintained the same way that insulin must be maintained for a diabetic. Deciding to stop the insulin after having a few good days isn't wise because eventually your body is going to wonder where that insulin is. At the end of the day, you need it to survive. The same goes for God. To treat the fear, start with following Philippians 4:6-9. Give your worries to God and focus on what is good, and God's peace will be with you. And then make a preventative care plan that includes plenty of stillness and more room for joy.

When you maintain your faith every single day, you can guarantee that God is going to increase your joy quotient and you truly will be stronger, braver, and more joyFULL no matter what season you are in!

Make It Personal

Has fear ever interrupted your life and postponed your dreams without consulting you?

Without judgment for yourself

I challenge you to take a beat and get curious about what dormant infections of fear and doubt might be waiting to erupt in your life. Write them down or shout them aloud while dancing around your room. Do you, friend! But please do it. Get real with your fear so that you can make a plan to address the root cause!

Now check in with yourself. How does it feel to reflect on fear? Is it depressing and overwhelming or invigorating and freeing? Either way, it's "normal" because it's your journey. No judgement here, just exploration, revelation, and growth.

What can you do **RIGHT NOW** to start treating you fear with faith? Just one thing!

Part 4

Room for Grief

Part 4: Room for Grief
The Beginning of Grief

Written in the middle of the mess....

Next to my love, I lay wondering if he still sees the beauty in my edges and curves. His distance isn't intentional—it is merely the repercussions of pain.

Grief has yet to take its full course. A small piece of us has transformed into joy, but there is another side that is vexed and vicious. It is this side of grief that is hard to live with.

Is this the edge of despair? How close can one get without falling over?

I sense his disappointment in life's hand—I make this personal {because it is} and let myself take ownership over the disappointment.

Here things begin to die —
Dreams. Hope. Love.

Grief and pain are complicated, and even worse, they will sneak up on you. They arrive uninvited, and when you are least prepared—they're those guests who show up unannounced, have already had too much to drink, and are fully ready to make a scene. They choose you because of the circumstances and experiences that you've had or are currently enduring. They mysteriously have complete access to your heart, soul, and mind. I have experienced plenty of losses. Still, the grief I was forced to wade through after meeting and marrying Lenny, a.k.a. Mr. Walker, almost destroyed me.

The cliché that everything happens for a reason is not lost on me. I was in remission from cancer when Mr. Walker and I met. God heard my requests and answered them perfectly. He knew that I needed to be released from the hurt that lingered from past betrayals and that I was firm about my "never dating again" policy. God also knew that I was going to need a partner, a friend who was mature enough in his faith to take on the recurring tidal wave of crisis, which was unfortunately scheduled to hit again.

I remember the first time Lenny and I had dinner together, just the two of us. We barely knew each other but ended up going to the opera together. I had received last-minute tickets from a friend and offered them up on Facebook. Lenny was the first person to respond and thus began the creation of God's very own Hallmark-like movie romance just for me. Instead of the flowery edited made-for-TV version, mine is uncut and includes all the messed-up parts! So, there we were, alone in this restaurant on a cold winter's night, eating, drinking, and laughing. WOW—this felt good. It had been a long time since I sat with a man on a Saturday night and felt at ease.

My smile wasn't forced, and the armor I had been wearing to protect my heart felt a bit heavy and unnecessary. That night, out of nowhere, I looked up across the small dimly lit table and a bowl of guacamole and said, "You know what? I think we are going to be really good friends." He quickly responded, "I think so too." God did something that night. I was totally unaware of it, but this was the beginning of my next chapter. Lenny and I began to message each other in the mornings during the *Today* show—we love us some Al Roker—and we'd check in with each other in the evenings too.

Lenny was there on the other end of the phone line to listen to me the day that my boss abruptly announced that she was planning on letting me go. I was fearful and distraught. Once again, I felt unappreciated and disposable. We talked that night for hours like we were teenagers. He listened and seemed to offer more measured advice—he didn't indulge my tendency to dive deeply into the pool of victimhood. He provided a lovely reliable balance to my fear. He helped me to see that not everything is as it seems and that if God still wanted me at my job, then He would make a way. It was easy to be hopeful around Lenny. And the truth is Lenny was right. God had always provided for me, and He wasn't about to stop. I didn't end up losing my job, and it even eventually expanded.

We started hanging out all the time. Lenny became my plus one to work events and miraculously got me out of the house on weeknights to attend Broadway shows. He was quickly becoming my faith-based comic relief and the friend that increased my joy quotient. He wasn't fazed by the fact that I was in such a complicated relationship, estranged from my husband, and not yet divorced.

He was respectful and always platonic in his body language and demeanor. There were no ulterior motives to this friendship, and that felt comforting. I'd never been around a man who was so genuine and honest. And believe me, Mr. Walker is brutally honest. Lenny is the type of man that, for better or worse, says exactly what he is thinking—all of the time. He warned me about this when we became friends and said, "I always go for the 'funny,' and because of that, at some point, I will offend you or hurt your feelings." Lenny was setting himself up for success by setting my expectations! You see how that works?

One of the first things that united us was food. We love eating it and talking about it. Entertaining and cooking have forever been passions of mine. My dad said that when I was little, I always wanted to go to fancy restaurants with tablecloths. I also had a habit of inviting people from our church over for Sunday dinner without talking to my parents first. My mom loved that! I guess I have always loved a dinner party. It made sense that when my first husband ended up in the restaurant industry, I was initially pleased. This gave me ample opportunity to try out new recipes and host plenty of dinner parties.

Cooking and entertaining seemed to give me a purpose and increase my self-worth. Many adoptees find themselves as adults in situations where they are continuously trying to be helpful. I learned later through years of therapy that much of this has do with our innate fear of being rejected. If I could be the best cook, the best entertainer, and the best wife, then maybe I would be worthy of love and acceptance.

Unfortunately, my passion and love for entertaining had been tarnished by betrayal. I'd barely entertained or even cooked since my then-husband severed ties. But now, I had the opportunity to reignite that passion and gift of hospitality on different terms—my own! It turned out that Lenny had a good friend, someone who had become like a little sister to him, and she was going through some "stuff." You know, the kind of "stuff" that we all go through in our twenties as we are searching for love, acceptance, and purpose. Not that age matters for the "stuff" we go through. I still find myself searching for those things sometimes!

As Lenny and I talked more about her, he thought my influence might be useful. He asked if he could invite her over for dinner one Sunday evening. This act would prove to solidify our bond and become the foundation for our non-dating courtship. That month, our Sunday dinner family was formed. For the next six months, Lenny, myself, our little "sister," and one of our best friends would meet for dinner. We eventually named ourselves the DeLattes because we all have a different ethnic makeups and a unique shade. I am the Vanilla Spice Latte, Lenny is the Carmel Macchiato, Ebo is the Mocha Latte, and Lex is the Cinnamon Dolce Latte. I know, we are strange. We are four people from totally different upbringings that surprisingly fit perfectly together. We are 'framily' (Friend + Family)! We each bring uniquely fabulous puzzle pieces to the table that create the most beautiful picture.

Anyway, every Sunday I would cook, and we would laugh and talk and grow. God used those months to show me that I was not the only broken one in this world. It may sound silly, but I was relieved that everyone had something they needed support and healing from. We all have gremlins—fears, doubts, and insecurities that prevent us from stepping into the joy, peace, and love that God is surrounding us with. As we routinely squeezed around my tiny Brooklyn table in an apartment that was the size of some people's closets, our love for each other, ourselves, and our faith multiplied.

During that time, my feelings toward Lenny also began to shift. The parts of my heart which I thought were irreparable and dead began to spark back to life. What was this feeling, and why was I feeling it? I was not interested in a relationship because I was not interested in giving someone total access to my heart again. I did not trust that I could ever be loved, desired, and cherished by anyone other than God. And I wasn't even confident in that somedays. But God! Despite my reluctance to give my heart away to another man, I was having these annoying feelings and because of Lenny's demeanor, I was getting no indication that He felt the same way.

Plus, I still wasn't officially divorced yet. That is an entirely different storyline—one fraught with division, anger, hurt, and frustration. My mom told me that I just needed to pray and trust God. Um ... that is not what I wanted to hear. Didn't you get the memo, mom? I wanted YOU to tell me that I could do something. She insisted that God had a plan and that my only job was to continue to seek Him and wait for Him to turn the page. I hate waiting. Yes, I *know*, hate is a strong word. But for real, does anyone love waiting for suffering, pain, or uncertainty to end? And historically, God doesn't give us much indication of just how long we might be expected to wait. It's not like when you call customer service for something, and although it might be annoying, they do at least tell you how long you will be on hold. But even though God may not reveal His timeline, He does set our expectations. He promises in Isaiah 40:31 that "those who wait, trust, and hope in the LORD will find new strength. They will soar high on wings like eagles. They will run and not grow weary. They will walk and not faint." The customer service line may tell us how long we have to wait before speaking with someone, but they don't promise us a positive outcome. Only God does that.

There I was, waiting for God to give me permission; it was hard, but it was also wonderful. Each day, my faith increased and my fear decreased. God was reconfiguring my heart and soul. God was using this time to answer the other requests I had presented to Him so long ago—to prepare my heart, mind, and spirit to love again. His timing would prove to be perfect.

Remember how I told you that Lenny says funny, yet totally inappropriate and often hurtful things sometimes? Well, one Sunday evening, he jumped right into that truth! We had finished eating, and everyone was gone except for him and me. He leaned back onto my couch, rubbed his belly, and said, "What are you trying to do? Make me fat so that no one will want to be with me, and I will have to marry you?" Really? I mean, this was a complete foot-in-mouth moment. I know some of you might be chuckling right now, and truthfully when I tell this story, I get a good laugh too because this is classic Lenny Walker. Yet, back when this happened, I was so fragile and afraid of being hurt that this response really stung. I remember being taken aback and warm with anger, but I let it slide ... for a few hours.

I filed my annoyance and was definitely not going to let it go completely. Much later that evening, I sent a long and pointed message to Lenny. It went something like this: *Lenny, when we first met, I told you that I had a difficult time letting people get close to me. But you and I now have an intimate friendship, and I am extremely hurt by what you said tonight. I don't want to hold you back from anything or anyone. So please do not think that is the case.*—SEND. A few moments passed, and I know now that Lenny was frantically trying to figure out how to respond via message. He realized that it was time to have "the conversation"—the scary one, which requires you to risk being hurt for the hope of being loved.

My phone rang, and I answered with a slight chill in my voice. Lenny spoke slowly and timidly, "Hey, Um ... I'm sorry ... I warned you that at some point, my words would hurt you. But, the truth is .... I like you. I have feelings for you." SILENCE. I couldn't speak, which was astonishing because I always have something to say. Finally, I blurted out, "I hope you know the feeling is mutual!" That was it. There was an enormous mutual sigh of quiet relief, and it was beautiful.

I went to bed that night with a smile on my face but woke up in a panic. I was still not officially divorced, and Lenny didn't know. How was I going to tell him this? After so many years of suffering, I was ready for an extended dance break! I was desperate for the kind of joy that makes people jump up and down! You know, like the time Tom Cruise jumped all over Oprah's couch?! I called my mom and asked her to pray. Of course, she was not worried; she never is.

My lawyer had filed the papers long before this date, but there seemed to be a holdup getting the divorce finalized. That morning, my emotions fluctuated between elation and anxiousness. And then my phone rang; it was my lawyer. I was surprised to hear from her because she was actually on vacation. She received a strange letter in the mail from the Brooklyn courthouse regarding my case, so she drove into the city to check on the filing in person. Turns out, my divorce was finalized two weeks prior, but she was just finding out that day. Wow! God's timing is always perfect and right on time. The next night after prayer meeting, Lenny drove me home and said, "I guess we should go on a date now ... but it kind of feels like we have already been dating for seven months and just didn't realize it!" He was right.

We had been dating since that very first post-opera dinner. God heard all of my requests, and He hears yours too. It might feel like He has stopped listening or that He doesn't care about your feelings or future. Even though that is not true, those emotions are still normal, valid, and hard to manage. This is why faith and hope are so important.

I had fallen in love with Lenny. Still, the lingering possibility that cancer would return prevented me from fully embracing the excitement of this new relationship. I knew Lenny loved me. Nevertheless, before starting a life together, I needed him to commit to all of me—the healthy version, the sick version, and the potentially infertile version. I wanted to believe that God had a plan for my chemo–damaged ovaries, but I knew there was a chance that they couldn't produce the eggs needed to have babies. I couldn't bear to be left again and wanted to give Lenny a way out before handing over too much of my heart and soul to him.

The wounds from past rejections were not yet healed, and I was still susceptible to the infections of fear and doubt. Trusting God felt impossible at times. Around this time, one of the DeLatte's—Cinnamon Dolce—had a meaningful chat with Lenny. Most people knew of his desire to have a family. This was something that he spoke about openly. She asked, "How do you truly feel about the fact that Vanessa might not be able to have kids?" He answered, "I love her more than I love the idea of having a family. Vanessa is more important to me than having biological children. God chose her for me, and I choose her too." When I heard about this conversation, my heart melted, and I shed yet another piece of that heavy armor that had been guarding my heart for so long.

You know, there is nothing wrong with guarding your heart. In fact, God tells us that it is precisely what we should do. God says to "guard your heart—above all else—for everything you do flows from it." (Proverbs 4:23) I love the way the author and leadership expert Michael Hyatt explains why guarding your heart is essential. He explains that our hearts are valuable, our hearts are the source of everything we do, and our hearts are under constant attack. He concludes by saying, *"If your heart is unhealthy, it threatens everything else—family, friends, career—everything!"*

When we don't guard our hearts, our feelings can take the lead when it comes to making important decisions. Decisions like who we should let into our lives and who we should keep out. If these emotions are rooted in peace and love, then that might be okay, but often our feelings are rooted in fear, doubt, and uncertainty. Decisions that flow from those emotions do not usually end up being the best choices. Believe me, I know! This is why intimacy with life partners or close friends is so special. Intimacy requires us to let our guard down so they can participate with us in the most vulnerable and transparent ways. If Lenny and I were going to work, then I needed to let my guard down and show him my heart. This leap of faith took major courage! It felt like I was a bungee jumping off one of the tallest bridges in the world. It was scary and exhilarating.

Fifteen months later, Lenny and I tied the knot. It was a perfect day. We entered into the marriage full of faith, and similar to many people in their mid-thirties, we had our minds focused on starting a family together. Before we said, "I do," we knew there was a chance that my cancer could return, but that was certainly the furthest thing from our minds.

I was on a medication that prevented me from getting pregnant, but I had seen God do so much in the last few years, and my faith had increased. God had provided me a man who was full of integrity, patience, and positivity. Mr. Walker is a glass-half-full kind of guy, which proves to be a valuable trait, given my ultra-realistic and glass-half-empty narrow view of life sometimes. I was convinced that this was the beginning of my season of fullness—whatever that means. In my mind, I thought suffering had ended. But the end of pain never happens. There will always be another difficulty or crisis. That is life.

We were just settling into the glow of newlywed life when the dreaded news was revealed. Cancer. Again. I found myself newly married, coming out of a challenging time of brokenness, assuming God was going to propel me to the next season, and now I had cancer! I was also informed by the doctors that I have a genetic mutation, which can lead to more cancer and, in fact, might kill me someday. This was not what I was hoping for from this new season of fullness. It felt like we'd been body-slammed by disappointment.

Unfortunately, accepting the possibility of sickness and infertility does not prepare you for the devastation attached to the reality of those things coming to pass. When we found ourselves knee-deep in the mess of cancer and questionable fertility, how we dealt with the uncertainty and pain differed. For me, the way I looked at pregnancy began to morph. My understanding of the miracle of life didn't match the world's view anymore. The joy and excitement that were supposed to be a part of becoming a mom were now replaced with fear, sadness, and anger. I also carried around an incredible amount of guilt. I believed this whole situation was my fault. Once again, cancer interrupted my life and began to bury my hope beneath the shards of my shattered dreams.

After my first cancer, the doctors told me that my treatments might make having children difficult in the future. But, back then, I didn't have the spiritual energy to even think about kids. My relationship was fractured, my heart and soul were battered, and my ability to dream had come to an abrupt halt. As I bounced from doctor to doctor, their recommendations became like a blur. I was more focused on hoping that that first cancer would somehow force my then-husband back into loving me rather than figuring out the future of my fertility. I also didn't have anyone advocating for me. No one took me aside and said, "I know you are not thinking about kids right now, but the time will come when you will want a family. And when that time comes, you should have some pre-chemo eggs stored away." No one was there to remind me that someday I would dream again.

With that first cancer diagnosis still visible in life's rear view mirror combined with the present diagnosis and my faulty genetics, Lenny and I were faced with a bleak reality. After many doctor's appointments and plenty of prayers, the decisions were made. All that was left was the follow-through. Ovaries out, breasts gone, and new meds to combat the stubborn mutated cells that longed to take up permanent residency in my body.

What I didn't realize was that while we were focused on keeping me alive, grief was settling into the deepest parts of my heart and soul.

As it turns out, Angelina Jolie—you know, the famous actress—was also having her double mastectomies that winter as well. I guess this could have been comforting, but truthfully it was tough to watch her journey play out on TV. It wasn't that her pain or trauma was that different than mine, but seeing so much support for her while I was isolated and struggling made everything worse. It highlighted all the difficulties within my own reality. Angelia broke the news of her surgeries in a short op-ed piece, published in the *New York Times*. It was a very "personal" account of her journey and those of her mother and aunt, who sadly both lost their lives to cancer. I have spent enough time in hospital waiting rooms to know that cancer is no respecter of race, religion, gender, age, or socioeconomic status. It is happy to take up residency in anyone, and it seems that everyone has some connection to this disease. Perhaps this is the reason why so many people were compelled to talk about Angelina's article. As soon as the story broke, the news anchors, bloggers, and social media gurus quickly joined forces to bring awareness to hereditary and genetic breast cancer.

As the doctors and nurses who treated Angelina got prepped by PR professionals for their moment in the spotlight, I sat curled up on my pint-sized couch with my orange cat, a coffee brewed by Mr. Walker, and an ice pack close by to help with the pain from my most recent surgery. My hair was dirty, really dirty—greasy at the roots and frizzed out at the ends. I was just too tired to wash it. It was still difficult to lift my arms, scrub my scalp clean, and blow dry my own hair.

I did try at one point to teach Lenny how to use a diffuser, but quickly realized that if we continued with that beauty skills tutorial, our marital bliss might be in jeopardy! I still don't get how someone so smart couldn't grasp the instructions—scrunch with one hand and diffuse with the other? Anyway, I decided it was wise to "take one for the team" and sacrifice good hair days for a healthier marriage! Hair care was a job better suited to my girlfriends. Thank God for them!

The morning Angelina's story surfaced, I'm sure I was wearing a pair of well-worn pajama bottoms and an oversized shirt. I wasn't going to win any fashion awards with this outfit, but the comfy shirt slipped easily over my swollen torn-up chest, which was now the host of two extra-large saline holding cells. The doctors called these expanders, and they were placed under the fragile, irradiated skin that once covered my breasts. Those breasts that I was born with were now long gone. I assume after they had been divvied up and passed through the appropriate pathologists' scopes that the remaining tissue was simply discarded. Sad. Even though they did try to kill me—twice—I missed them. I still do.

The media frenzy surrounding Angelina's decision to have these surgeries and talk about them publicly would not die down after a few weeks, but instead would gain momentum and soon be labeled, "The Angelina Effect". This effect only intensified when she, like many with a BRCA mutation, made the difficult decision to have her ovaries removed as well. Just one more thing that we have in common.

When I tell people that I am a cancer patient, shock and a little disbelief is almost always their first response. This is often followed by an over-the-top compliment about how beautiful, strong and resilient I am. However, beneath these adulations, there is usually a sliver of fear. And, the questions keep coming—"What kind of cancer?" "Does it run in your family?" It seems that people are consciously (or subconsciously) trying to come up with a good reason for why I got cancer. If they can find blame somewhere it saves them from having to wonder if they too could be chosen as a host for this disease.

After Angelina's article, the final question would usually go something like this, "Oh, that's just like Angelina, right?"

Well, the short answer is no. I'm not just like Angelina, and although our journeys share some common elements, the thought that my years of cancer treatments were being compacted and simplified to provide a comparison to Angelina's journey was frustrating. Cancer was already hard to explain to outsiders. Now, I regularly had to explain how I differed from Angelina and why things seemed more difficult for me. Cancer may not be a respecter of race, gender, or class, but socioeconomic levels certainly factor into how someone deals with the realities of this disease. The financial burden alone is something that certainly separates the celebrity patient from the rest of us.

The day after the op-ed was published, I found myself writing a letter of response to Angelina. The feelings poured out of me with force, like water from a fire hose. It felt so good to reveal what was brewing in my heart and soul. I sent this letter to the *New York Times* as well as a few other media outlets which had been covering the "breast cancer crisis" with great vigor, but never received a response. Nothing. Just silence. It felt like no one really cared about my story. I knew at that moment that my voice would never hold the same kind of weight as my celebrity "sister".

I CRINGE A BIT WHEN I GO BACK AND READ THIS LETTER.

I choose to read it now and then so I can remember just how far I have come. The tone of victimhood resonates in the phrases and the bitter edge of the letter is dressed up with compliments and nicety. But the truth is I really just wanted to scream, "PLEASE SEE ME! Please see that I am different. This is hard ... so hard. I am angry, sad and jealous ... and I just want everyone to stop telling me how lucky I am to be alive! Stop comparing me to her. Just STOP!" It felt so complicated and messy and everyone was trying to make it more palatable so that it was easy to digest. But cancer is never easy to digest; it is always messy and always complicated. It just isn't something you can put into a box with an all-encompassing label.

Cancer is never easy to digest; it is always messy and always complicated.

Most of our journeys look nothing like those of our celebrity "friends". Back then I was longing to hear or read a more truthful, less romanticized version of cancer—one that conveyed the messy details of my story and the stories of the exhausted, regular, working-class men and women who sit with me in waiting rooms week after week.

I was grieving my hopes, my dreams, my breasts, and my fertility. Even now, it is hard for me to articulate this grief. Everything was gone, and what remained of my womanhood left me feeling desolate and barren. I'd always dreamt of having children, but trying to see past the tsunami of grief that just hit my household was impossible.

Years would pass before Mr. Walker and I had the spiritual courage and financial help to move toward trying to have a baby. My doctors had made it clear that carrying a child was not advisable for me. It turns out that hormones feed my cancer, so pregnancy was really out of the question! Thankfully, Lenny and I had two beautiful embryos safely frozen and just waiting for us to let them out, but I was terrified. It was much easier to keep the possibility of my children protected than allow another opportunity for me to be disappointed. Friends and family continued to ask us what we were going to do, and we always had the same answer: "We are waiting for God to give us peace and open a door."

You have to understand, when Lenny and I were first married our immediate goal was to get my doctors on board with letting me off my current cancer drugs so that we could try and have a baby. I had been on an adjuvant therapy for about four years—that just means I took a cancer prevention pill everyday—but to have a baby I needed to go off those meds. My doctors were hesitant but also understood my desire to live my life. This is one thing that I cherish about my medical team.

Often my surgical oncologist, Dr. John Kehoe, says to me, "OK, let me take off my doctor hat and put on my regular person hat." He knows that sometimes it's important to look at the whole person, not just the disease—someone with dreams, hopes and desires. He knew that every decision I made wasn't always going to line up exactly with what I "should" be doing if we were just thinking about the cancer. Please do not underestimate the importance of this! When you have cancer, many doctors and regular people see the cancer first instead of looking past the disease to see the person as well. I was desperate to have a baby that was part Vanessa Joy and part Lenny Ray! The doctors agreed to let Lenny and I do one round of IVF before my surgeries. This was a big decision, because everyone knew that the drugs that were needed to harvest my eggs contained the same hormones that my type of cancer seemed to thrive on. I went to see a specialist at NYU who worked with high-risk cancer patients like myself, and she set my expectations. She said, "Chemotherapy and cancer-related hormone treatments have already significantly decreased you chances to harvest eggs. Normally I would not take on a case like yours, but seeing as this is your last hope, we might as well go for it!" At this point Lenny and I were so prayed up that we were positive God was going to open all of the doors that were needed to get this party started.

Truthfully, it wasn't much of a party—daily needles, more than normal moodiness, and that constant fear cancer might spread loomed heavy. We were, however, surprisingly upbeat. We actually look back on that time and laugh a lot. It was a regular comedy of errors every time Lenny had to jab me in the behind or belly. I remember one time in particular that I squirmed or yelped, and he pulled the needed out before completing the injection. I started screaming, and he couldn't understand why. I was like, "Dude, you've got to follow through! Be bold and courageous, my friend." But my favorite memory was when we both got the twenty-four-hour stomach flu on a day we had to go to the clinic. Lenny gave me my morning shot, and shortly after that I started puking. About twenty minutes later, he started vomiting, and I moved on to diarrhea … yes, folks, this is real life. Back then, our apartment was so small that the refrigerator was in the living room! This was true NYC living. We only had one bathroom and one small kitchen sink. Have you seen the movie *Bridesmaids*? This was a real "It's happening" moment! Please note that somewhere between the puking and pooping we also had to drive into the city to the clinic. This required us to switch seats at stop lights so that we could take turns vomiting in a grocery bag in the car. Please take a moment to visualize me running around a big red truck in Brooklyn, NY with vomit in my hair … All I will say is that the WHOLE apartment (and car) had to be disinfected after that ordeal. It was a real mess—literally. Sorry, was that TMI (too much information)?

The good news is that each ultrasound exceeded our expectations and surprised my doctors. I was starting to create eggs! On the day of my egg retrieval we said one last prayer and went to the clinic to do our respective business (enough said). That day two whispers of life were formed—Walker embryo #1 and Walker embryo #2.

Just a quick reminder, all of that happened BEFORE my mastectomies and before I had my ovaries out. By the time I was in remission and we could think about HOW to bring these whispers into the world, we were already exhausted! God would need to move a whole mountain range to get us to the place of parenthood.

Prayers went up for years, but nothing seems to come down. Sure we heard from God on other things, but not on this. We had no direction and no peace about what to do next. And then finally one day a deacon from my church called me up and said that I had been on her mind. She had recently met a Christian couple who used a gestational carrier to have a baby. She thought that we might want to explore that option. This was another one of those BUT GOD moments. Lenny and I both had complete peace, and within a weeks we had set up a call to discuss the process, and a close friend had offered us a substantial gift to help cover the costs.

A few short months later, we had a carrier and were well on our way to having our babies! I was so excited. I started looking at baby clothes and saving photos of nursery decor. We even began looking for a larger apartment to accommodate a few little ones. We really wanted a kitchen that could fit a refrigerator! It was so wonderful to finally have something to look forward too. This was the first time in a very long time that I almost felt "normal." The contract process was a breeze and the dates were set up for the implantation. Yes! This was really happening. EEK. I am smiling as I write this because it brings back such wonderful memories.

When you experience significant trauma, it can feel like pain and disappointment are the norm. So when a glimmer of hope appears and things start turning around, it is even more devastating when that hope train runs off the rails. You just can't help but wonder, WHY is this happening to me?

Lenny and I experienced this one July morning just a few weeks away from our implantation appointment. Our caseworker called and her voice was noticeably shaky and abnormally quiet: "We just received word that your gestational carrier's family was in a horrible car accident. Her sixteen-year-old daughter and sister were killed."—"What? This couldn't be happening. We were so close. Why God? WHY GOD?" My body felt weak. My mind raced and the questioning ramped up, "Will nothing EVER work out for me?" It didn't take but a second for the guilt to flood in. How could I be thinking about myself when this women's life was just totally devasted? How could I be thinking about my own dreams when hers had just evaporated? The complications of this situation are impossible to capture. I could barely function for weeks.

Then about a month later, in the middle of my own disappointment, God put this woman on my heart. I decided to travel to meet up with her. Despite us not sharing that baby experience together, we were still connected. I remember embracing her in the middle of a Starbucks coffee shop in a small town in North Carolina. She wept quietly and time stood still. It was clear from this meeting that she did not have the kind of spiritual support that was needed to get through these initial months, so I began to call and text her daily to encourage her and check in. You know this is a clear example of how sometimes God takes our purpose in a whole new direction. I thought this woman came into my life to help ME, but truthfully I was there to help her.

More months would pass before I could even begin to think about trying to find a new surrogate. Lenny and I fought about what to do next, and I yelled a lot at everyone.

I was weak, exhausted, overwhelmed, and desperate for something good to happen. That is when we were introduced to our dear angel. I will call her Deena. She was a true answer to prayer. God always shows up right on time. Within five minutes of our first call, we both knew that God had been saving her for us! We moved quickly to get everything in order, and this time it was seamless. She instantly became family. God was doing something in our lives and we couldn't really figure out what it was, but we were thrilled to be on this journey together. Soon it was time to for the implantation!

On a cold blustery day in February, we were all welcomed to Connecticut with some sad news. One of our whispers wasn't growing and could not be saved. Strangely, I was sad but not devastated. I knew in my heart that God was planning to do something beautiful with the one whisper that was still with us. I get warm fuzzy feelings as I remember watching the doctor implant Whisper #1—seeing him place all our hopes into its new home for the next nine months was incredibly beautiful. It was finished! Now all we had to do was wait! This may have literally been the longest few weeks of my life.

And then we got the call—the one that every expectant parent waits for—"You're pregnant!" This was happening, and it was happening to me. My dreams were finally coming true. Every day I eagerly waited for text messages and pictures from Deena chronicling her every move. Then weeks into the pregnancy, Deena's blood work came back indicating a complication. But at this point, I couldn't entertain the thought of this not working. Why would God let us come all this way just to have it end in disaster? Sure, I was on edge, but so many people were praying, This was my miracle!

A few weeks later, at a clinic on the other side of the country, our surrogate sat keeping our whisper of life safe—praying and singing over her belly. Together we're believing that on this day, our past mourning and suffering would instantly turn to joy. Mr. Walker and I didn't talk much that morning, because there were no words left to say and no prayers left to pray. God's miracles had been woven into every part of our journey, and we were familiar with the cadence of "wait and pray." So that is what we did. The phone rang, and Deena, the guardian of our whisper of life, appeared on the screen—she was glowing. This was the moment we all expected to experience a miracle of God in the sound of a tiny heartbeat. Instead, that day, our hope turned to pain, and our pain turned to grief. The silence was deafening. It still is.

I had suffered before and was accustomed to disappointment, but this was different. This pain rushed in like a flood—devastating the landscape of my soul. I instantly felt alone in my own desolate land, surrounded by those shards of broken dreams and fractured hopes. That faith, which had carried me through many severe crises, evaporated so quickly that it was hard to imagine it had ever existed in the first place. The tears flowed, but the weeping was silent. There was not a groan deep enough to release the grief I was experiencing.

The day we found out that our baby was gone is etched in my soul. We had already been through so much. The road from cancer diagnosis, through many surgeries and treatments, to IVF and surrogacy was a long one. It was exhilarating and exhausting—full of highs and lows. After years of praying and seeking after God's will, we had arrived at this crossroads. We had waited patiently and clung to the hope that God would not bring us this far to disappoint us. How could He? This was going to be the exclamation point to our testimony.

This was the beginning of a new foreign strain of grief, one that I was not yet prepared to embrace and certainly could not understand. It was messy and layered. All of my disappointments and losses were converging and transforming into one enormous life-threatening, heart-wrenching virus. I couldn't figure out where it started, and I didn't think it would ever end. Recovering from this grief would require a full and intense treatment plan.

Have you ever experienced a soul-crushing loss that it makes fresh the pain of every past wound and disappointment? A crisis that forces you to question everything? A situation devastating enough that even the memories of past blessings are blocked by a wall that is impossible to see through?

It's easy to trust God when you are in the middle of a blessing or when you've prayed for something that's totally impossible and God has shown up. But you know, the truth is that sometimes we cry out to God with everything in us, asking Him for something that's deep in our hearts, and then the answer shows up in a way that is contrary to what we think God is supposed to do. It's devastating and disorienting. Often, we imagine what our testimonies are supposed to look like, and we begin writing the final chapters to our own stories. We push ahead of God and decide to choose our own ending, but God's conclusions are so much better than any end we could ever wish or imagine for ourselves.

At this point, things were out of control. This loss shook my faith in a way that cancer, divorce, and everything else I had endured had not done. I cried out to God. I wasn't just distraught over the grief, but I was worried that I might lose my faith because if there's one thing I know, a life without God is no life at all. I didn't want to live my life without hope and separated from God. The alternative to believing in God is to be alone with no one to cry out to in times of trouble. There would be no assurance that God would take all the things ... not just the good stuff, and not only these prayers answered in the way we want them answered ... but everything and turn it into something beautiful.

I was just stepping into the grief. I had yet to figure out how I was going to get out of it. And that is okay. All I had to do was grasp tightly to that mustard seed of faith and choose to believe.

Is grief in your view?

Are you in the middle of a struggle? Have you lost a loved one, a relationship, or a dream? Are you in a place where the sky is dark and the storm is so massive that you feel like you can't reach out? Trust me, God is there. He is as close as the mention of His name. God's got you, even if you can't feel Him, He is holding on to you. If you are in the beginning stages of your grief, be kind to yourself. Be intentional about encouraging yourself.

I am betting that depending on the day, I could ask you to define grief and get very different answers. When it comes to grief, it's easy to feel discouraged. Emotions are intense, and those are one of the hardest things we will ever work to rein in. I often think about what cancer, infertility, and past betrayals have stolen from me. Has the world stolen precious things from you? There isn't a day that goes by that I don't imagine what it would be like to carry my own child and look into the eyes of someone who grew in my belly. Why was I abandoned and betrayed so many times? Why did cancer choose me and steal so much from me and everyone who loves me?

I used to think that I could just wait for grief to disappear. That one day, I would wake up and it would be gone forever. Joy and hope would overflow and replace all the sadness and sorrow. Finally, I would be able to move on. I sensed that my friends and family were also waiting for grief to just go away—evaporate. I was irritable, emotional, and not much fun. It's not easy to be around the complicated, unflattering, and vicious side of grief. The fact that it still lingers is uncomfortable.

This part of grief is hard to live with, hard to be friends with, and hard to love. If you are waiting for grief to disappear in your life or someone else's life, you're in for a long wait. Grief doesn't evaporate, it transforms—*if* you give it some room to breathe. When grief is not allowed to breathe, then transformation and growth are impossible. Your grief becomes stagnant, like standing water in your inner being—growing moldy and toxic, creating an almost uninhabitable environment. The stench of pain rises and its power to overtake one's soul becomes greater than the crisis that created it. In this state, everything dies. There is no hope left, growth is impossible, and survival is questionable.

Grief doesn't evaporate, it transforms— *if* you give it some room to breathe.

I'm familiar with this uncomfortable place. Many times, I have tried to manage grief all on my own—never asking for help. I've been embarrassed and ashamed, afraid to acknowledge the deep pain that I am experiencing because everyone (including myself) is tired of walking the miserable road of loss that seems to have no end. The temptation to simply pretend grief doesn't exist is strong. Isn't the "joy of the Lord" I talk about supposed to replace the pain and make the uncertainty more manageable? Some moments, I forget that suffering is a part of the purpose. I forget that those who put their trust in God will not be ashamed. It is easy to forget when we are questioning and waiting that it is during those moments that God will strengthen and reveal Himself to us.

> *Those who put their trust in God will not be ashamed.*

Don't rush yourself or anyone else through the process of grief. Trying to answer grief with anything but love, space, and grace will inevitably add to the stagnancy and stench that grows because of its containment. Instead, open a window and let the breath of God waft in. Embrace the struggle. It is in this embrace that transformation happens, and we find ourselves ready and even excited for the questions, "What now?" and "What next?"

Are you ready to see what is next?

Make It Personal

Is grief in your view? Are you in the middle of a struggle? Have you lost a loved one, a relationship, or a dream?

Without judgment for yourself

I challenge you to get real with your grief. I am not going to give you any how-to prompts this time because this is so personal and intimate. **Now check in with yourself.** How does it feel to make room for grief? To give grief its own room to breathe?

What can you do **RIGHT NOW** to make enough space in your life for grief and God?

"I'm Not Okay! Okay?"

"We must start to shed the shame that surrounds not being okay."
—Hannah Rose, LCPC, Psychology Today

It's okay to not be okay. Read that again.

I know I am bossy—it is one of my spiritual gifts! But please read it slowly and let it sink in. Do you really believe that statement?

This is a statement that you don't hear enough in "faith-based circles." It's actually something we don't hear enough in any sphere. Sure, there might be Instagrammable quotes indicating that it is acceptable to have an off day—but is it really okay?

Are we ready to handle that icky, awkward, and uncomfortable vibe that usually surrounds disappointment, frustrations, sadness, and pain? Are we prepared for our most upbeat, positive friends to wear the ugly side of grief and be less adaptable than they usually are? Are we ready and willing to give to others in need without expecting anything in return? Suffering is ugly, unbearable, and full of agony. It's pretty apparent that if it were easy to be around, then it wouldn't be suffering. There seems to be this idea that people of faith should float above every negative situation with some sort of unexplained euphoria. That's simply not reality. Nor is it fair to those struggling daily to just barely make it. Life is messy for everyone. It is more than time for us to accept that truth and offer the extra grace that we owe ourselves and that others need as well.

I remember having a conversation with my boss while I was finishing out my radiation treatments during my first bout with cancer. I had become accustomed to apologizing all the time for things that were totally out of my control. I heaped guilt on myself for needing more time to complete tasks or for requiring extra rest. At work and church and with friends and family, I found myself apologizing for what I was going through. I was weak, vulnerable, and fragile. I mean, I had just gone through more than one surgical procedure and multiple types of chemo. Plus, I was getting up early every day before work to go to the hospital for radiation. Yet still, for some reason, I felt as though I needed to apologize. My boss and I were chatting on the subway about expectations when I had an "aha" moment and blurted out, "I've decided to stop apologizing for my crisis and my disease."

Let's be clear; she wasn't really asking me to apologize, but I did feel the constant need to say, "I'm sorry" to her and to everyone else in my life. It was a turning point for me to admit that some days—most days—were not that great, and it was okay because the situation was far from ideal. Being a Christian or a naturally upbeat person doesn't require you to spend all of your energy forcing yourself to float above the pain, and it's unrealistic to think that you can do that consistently. Sustaining that level of positivity is exhausting. I know, because I have tried to do this! Sometimes you need to give into the weakness so that God can show Himself strong. There is a purpose in your suffering, but you won't find that purpose until you are willing to recognize that the pain is part of the process.

Receive it, accept it, and walk in it. Dare I say, "Embrace it"? Remember, It's not your responsibility to romanticize pain or gloss over suffering for the sake of those around you. Convincing yourself that there's something wrong with the fact that you're

There is a purpose in your suffering, but you won't find that purpose until you are willing to recognize that the pain is part of the process.

having a difficult time will exhaust you. Maybe you're facing a divorce, betrayal, infertility, or illness, or perhaps you are tormented by a dream or a calling that hasn't taken form yet. To step into your purpose and make yourself available for God's use, you must be willing to get real, be vulnerable, and allow people to see that you're not okay.

When you give yourself the freedom to say, "I'm not okay today," a refreshing energy washes over you. It's like jumping into a slightly chilly pool on a hot summer's day. You instantly feel better. It also demonstrates to the people around you that they, too, don't have to act like everything is fine. Your actions grant them permission to yell, "I'm not okay, either." Honestly, so many of us are still waiting for permission to admit how we really feel. You have the ability to encourage that freedom in others when you accept it for yourself.

It won't be perfect. There will be situations that you won't know how to handle. Maybe you'll have a friend who is struggling in their marriage or with grief, or perhaps a coworker will be diagnosed with cancer. The possibilities of crises are endless, and knowing precisely what to say or how to react is complicated. Unless you've walked the exact road of the person who is suffering (which is impossible), then you won't know what to say. That's normal, and it's okay. Embracing this concept makes room for so many more meaningful things in your life. If you choose not to accept this, then be prepared to spend most of your energy trying to make situations that are *not* okay, appear as if they are.

What's the point of glowing up your crisis to prove to yourself or to the world that everything is okay? Isn't that exhausting? *By the way ... Glow-up is a word the kids are using these days. It means the complete transformation of a person's appearance for the better—I love using the kids' lingo!* Sometimes, the best thing you can do is admit that everything is not okay. If you need help, ask for it. It takes courage to ask for help. If one of your life goals is to make an impact, then being on the receiving end of service will educate and equip you to better step into your calling. It's hard to know how to help if you've never needed help yourself. Getting comfortable asking for help is part of learning to be okay with not being okay.

When Mr. Walker and I suffered the devastation of losing our baby, I struggled to move on. I didn't just struggle. I couldn't move on. I was paralyzed. I felt like I was supposed to just get over it and accept that God's master plan didn't include me having a baby. What was the point in praying if God was going to continue to ignore me? How long was God going to throw obstacles in my path and torment me with unachievable dreams? It was time for me to finally accept that bad things were always going to happen to me. I didn't even want to be married anymore. Sure, I loved Lenny, but I didn't want to be around anyone or anything that reminded me of how messed up, broken, and useless I was. What made it worse was I had nothing to offer him—I couldn't give him the family he longed for, I was miserable to be around, my body was scarred, and menopause had stolen my sex drive. I sincerely believed that I would be doing him a favor if I left. Friends tried to get me to go back to therapy, but I didn't want to talk to anyone. People began to notice my personality shift—I was less upbeat and more critical. It felt like everyone was waiting for me "get over it," and I just wanted to sit down in 'it' and disappear. Once again, I wanted to die. I didn't want to kill myself, but I did want God to give me cancer again so I could stop fighting and give in to death.

It was time for me to finally accept that bad things were always going to happen to me.

I knew that other people lost babies as well, and I wanted to believe that God's plan was good even though I could not understand it, but I was struggling. I didn't want to choose joy—I just wanted to curl up in a ball and cry all day. Many days, I did. I didn't want someone to tell me it was going to be okay, and I just needed to have faith. I wanted someone to say, "Hey, this totally sucks, and it's okay that you're struggling right now." I needed someone to cry with me and eat Magnolia Bakery's banana cream pie out of the tin with me. I needed someone to step into the pain with me before they tried to help pull me out of it.

In many ways, I've moved through the pain and grief that is intimately woven into infertility's journey and most days are better days. But sometimes I'm still not okay. There are moments when the reminders of this suffering seem to be everywhere. I don't have cute baby photos to post on Instagram or the ability to engage in conversations about child care with my peers. I continually have to defend why Mr. Walker and I have yet to adopt and act as if I am happy about the fact that I am cancer-free but childless. Plus, society has a way of quietly making people who don't have kids feel like they shouldn't need time off for themselves. It is as though having a passion that is not directly related to rearing a child is somehow self-serving or frivolous. And then there is Mother's Day—UGH. That is a complicated day for me. I'm adopted, so on this day, I am grieving my first mom, whom I never *really* met and is now dead. Plus, I am often away from my second mom— my heart—Elsie. I am also reminded that God knit me together with mutated cells which caused cancer, damaged my ovaries, and prevented me from ever having biological children.

Growing up, Mother's Day was an important holiday, especially at church. Children sang, and floral corsages—that walked the line of tasteful and tacky—were pinned to pastel lapels. Potted plants and bouquets were gifted to the oldest moms, mothers with the most children, and sometimes the soon-to-be moms.

Sadly, no one ever mentioned the young women who were trying to become mothers but couldn't seem to carry a baby to full term or single women who longed to be called mommy. I'm sure they often spent each day leading up to Mother's Day feeling significant sadness and loss. No one ever mentioned the mothers who willfully or because of difficult circumstances relinquished the care of their children to other people through adoption or foster care. What kind of unimaginable grief must they experience on this day meant in love and appreciation? We certainly never talked about infertility; that would be such a downer. This day was reserved for flowers, cards, and all things lovely. Mother's Day was supposed to be a happy day. So why was it so hard?

It wasn't until I was emerging as an adult that the loveliness which surrounded this holiday began to suffocate me. I remember the first time I felt sad and embarrassed on this special day. I was only twenty-four years old and in year three of marriage to my first husband.

We were living far away from family as I worked on my graduate degree in music. My husband worked weekends, and that left me flying solo most Sundays. That day, I rose early and put on a lavender and white gingham shift dress—it was perfect for a day that I knew would be drenched in pastels. It was chilly outside, and as I drove alone to the church, I felt a pang of sadness. I had no mother with me—she was far away in Canada, I had no husband with me—he was working, and I had no children with me—they were just a quietly protected dream. As I entered the church, a jovial man greeted me with a single flower and wished me a happy Mother's Day. I calmly said, "I'm not a mother," and I waved my hand to indicate he should save that flower for someone more deserving. He pushed the flower back toward me and said, "Someday, dear, you will be a mother." I politely accepted the small gift and found a seat near the back of the church. With my face masked in smiles and contentment, I secretly wondered if he was right. Would I ever be a mother?

Having children was an issue in my first marriage. When my ex and I met, I was still a kid; having children was not on my radar. But as I got older, my desire to expand our family grew. I tried not to think or talk about it that much, hoping that one day God would answer my prayers and change my husband's heart, so we too would become parents.

Yet now I am married to a wonderful man who dreams of fatherhood, and I find myself asking God why I didn't meet him sooner before chemotherapy and cancer began to eat away at my fertility. Or before the doctors told me my best chance of living a long life involved removing the one thing that makes me feel like a real woman—my ovaries. Why would God let this amazing guy get stuck with a sick girl with broken ovaries? The truth is, I don't know. Have you ever had something taken away that left you with more questions than answers? Those questions can haunt us and leave us wondering what happens next?

I still attend church every Mother's Day and wait to honor the women around me who have been blessed with the gift of parenthood. But this day is always sprinkled with despair. The words of that jovial church greeter from so many years ago get louder as each Mother's Day approaches. "Someday, dear, you will be a mother." Once again, I wonder, "Will I?"

When you can acknowledge that things are not okay and accept that you may need some help getting through the trial, you set yourself up for success. After Mr. Walker and I lost our little whisper of hope, things were tough—REALLY tough. It began to feel like everything in my life was broken—my body, my dreams, and my relationship. But that wasn't the truth. This loss was hard for my husband and me, but we were not broken, and our marriage was not broken. We just weren't okay. We simply needed help.

No one is happy about suffering, and nobody's happy all of the time. No one is happy when they deal with divorce, rejection, cancer, or any kind of crisis. If someone told me they were delighted after a cancer diagnosis while in the middle of a divorce, I would advise them to see a therapist because there would be something wrong with that situation. You would be in severe denial if you were in a state of happiness during that mess. Freedom emerges when you accept that things aren't going well and can start being honest about the pain. And freedom makes room for joy and protects your peace.

> *Freedom emerges when you accept that things aren't going well and can start being honest about the pain.*

Working for Peace

By looking at advice columns and self-help books, it's easy to become convinced that experiencing peace is something that you really have to work hard to obtain. Meditating more, going on more vacations, reading more inspirational books, and having more alone time are not bad ideas. But working hard at them doesn't guarantee that you will be at peace. Understanding the gift of peace is essential to overcoming difficulties. Most joyful people that I know are also at peace, and most peaceful people have joy! It's funny how that works. Right? Thankfully, God has given us a clear roadmap to peace and He lays it all out in the fourth chapter of Philippians.

First, we are reminded to be full of joy in the Lord. Second, we are told to keep rejoicing while being considerate in all that we do. Then, we are instructed not to worry about ANYTHING. Ugh … "Really, God?"

I want you to really get this point. It isn't easy, and this is a hard one for me. I worry so much that you would think that it feels good! But instead of trying to work the worry away, God simply gives me something else to do instead—pray. So that's what I do. I follow these instructions carefully and I pray about everything! Praying all the time and about everything can seem like a lot. But God is always listening and He knows what we need before we ask. He is waiting for a willing heart. If you find that you can't articulate what you need because you are consumed by worry, remember that the Holy Spirit intercedes for you and even understands the unspoken desires hidden deep in your soul.

The last stop on the road to peace is gratitude. This one is simple. Just be thankful. Instead of focusing on all that hasn't happened yet, focus on that which has been done. We all have something to be grateful for. And then God promises that we will experience His peace—a peace that will exceed our understanding! A peace that has the power to guard our hearts and minds. I don't know about you, but that's the kind of peace I need! My mind has a way of running off in all sorts of wild directions, and I need something powerful to keep me in check! Don't spend time holding on to the notion that you have to figure out a way to make yourself seem okay in situations that are not okay. You will miss the opportunity to grasp the transformative peace that has already been woven into your circumstances. Follow the roadmap!

Please don't mask or deny what you're genuinely feeling; it will only prolong the pain and prevent you from settling into the peace and the joy that is available for you. Maybe you're like me and analyze everything, hoping to understand exactly why something is happening. Stop now! Please, learn from my mistakes. That will leave you frustrated because we don't always know the reasons why. I certainly don't understand why some people have babies, and some people have miscarriages. I don't know why some people get cancer and some people don't. I don't understand why some people can identify and live out their gifts immediately, while others seem to take a long time to be nurtured and come to fruition. The difference now is that I'm okay with not understanding it all. I don't need to know all of the reasons why something happens. I'm excited because this is where the beauty of it all comes together. When you accept the fact that life is a little messy and that you don't have to wrap your brain around it all, you'll experience freedom, peace, and joy.

It can be hard to admit that you're not okay, and even harder to disclose it to someone else. We have been conditioned to keep our pain to ourselves. Even in the church, when you're asked how things are, your go-to response is, "I'm okay" when you're honestly not okay at all. I am not saying you should bare your soul to everyone! You'll need to have discernment and be thoughtful about how much you share and who you share it with, but when you do share, be honest. Don't let the fear of what others think hold you back.

Let me share an example that I think will help you see what I mean. When I found out that the pregnancy with our surrogate was not going to make it to full term, I was at a complete loss. I had been praying for years and I believed with my whole heart that Mr. Walker and I were going to have a beautiful baby with my green eyes and his sense of style! It took us years and lots of hope before we reached the point of finally receiving the news that we were pregnant. Why would God take it away?

Despite my preference to stay at home, curled in a ball and repeating the phrase, "Why me?" I dragged myself to church. When you are hurting and you are angry with God, there will be people in your faith family that won't understand. Walking out of service, I ran into someone who had been praying for us. The usual how are you feeling conversation ensued. I answered, "I'm terrible, actually. I don't understand, and to be honest, I am pissed off at God." She was visibly taken aback, not just by my confession, but I am sure by my less than flowery language. Her response made me realize that you can't expect people to understand where you are in any moment of suffering. She responded, "You shouldn't be mad at God. He is faithful, and we know He has a plan." Now, I genuinely believe she intended to encourage me, but the impact of her words hurt me. There was a moment when I wondered if there was something wrong with me because I was so angry with God? When suffering hits those you love and you can't understand where they are in their journey, all you need to do is show up and be present. You don't need to explain why "it" happened. At this moment, my friend couldn't handle the reality of my disappointment. Why? Because it was an assault on her faith too. She had prayed and interceded on our behalf, and she was hoping for a different outcome as well.

God Can Handle It

I have an reliable truth for you. God can handle all of this stuff. Remember my friend Sarah who says that God is not intimidated by our fear? Let's add that God is also not intimidated by our anger or our lack of understanding. God is not threatened by our unbelief. He's not intimidated by the fact that we get upset and don't want to talk to Him anymore. Still, it can be uncomfortable for other people.

> *God is not threatened by our unbelief.*

If everything was okay all the time, how would we know that God is a God that answers prayer? How would we ever experience the kind of comfort that we can get only from God during a crisis? If everything was excellent all the time, we would forfeit the opportunity of experiencing the miracles of God that strengthen our faith, anchor our hope, and inform our purpose! There is nothing inspirational about a life without pain.

When you allow people to witness your vulnerability, you help them to see and embrace their own. You'll help them experience the freedom that results from being honest about how they feel. Others will be encouraged when they see you and hear you say, "This too shall pass, but right now it's rough. And I don't like it." You'll be better able to serve people because you're not trying to cover up a problem with a little lipstick or foundation. You show up without makeup, without a mask, and then give them permission to do the same.

One Sunday a few years ago, I ended up sitting next to a young woman who had just joined the choir at my church. As we began talking, I noticed she was a little standoffish. I asked her if she was married, and she curtly told me she was separated. I responded by letting her know that when I joined the choir, I was in the middle of a messy separation as well. I shared a little bit of my story and how difficult it was to come to church back then. Every Sunday I showed up, but felt like I didn't belong. I thought that if people knew how messed up my marriage was, they would judge me.

Years later, my friend told me from her perspective what happened that day. She said, "I remember sitting next to you and hearing you going on and on about your husband and how he did all these nice things for you. You were bubbly and seemed so happy. The last thing I wanted was to sit next to an upbeat woman who was talking about her great husband because mine had just left me. But then you told me how messed up your life had been when you first joined the choir. How uncomfortable it was and how you felt like you didn't belong. You put it all out there, and I was immediately at ease. It was such an encouragement to me."

Everyone knows that I talk too much and am probably a bit too transparent at times. But that Sunday, God knew what my friend needed to hear. How amazing it is that He used my messed-up life to shine a light into her corner of darkness and discouragement. All I had to do was show up unmasked and be friendly.

Sometimes you need to show others the ugly, uncertain, and messed-up versions of your life. We all need to know that we are not alone and that our pain or discouragement is valid. People need to know that light at the end of the tunnel exists even though they can't see or feel it at the moment.

> *Sometimes you need to show others the ugly, uncertain, and messed-up versions of your life.*

Surviving Crisis

A crisis can make you feel like you are in a dark tunnel, lost and stumbling with an almost nonexistent light to lead the way. Your transparency and willingness to share with others allows you to become the light in the middle of someone else's darkness. Once you've taken the path through a dark tunnel or two (or three), you know the way out. We may feel trapped sometimes, but God is never confined. He is moving around us, equipping us, and preparing us for our purpose. He has got you today. Choosing hope may feel uncomfortable and clumsy at times. It takes courage to step out into the unknown. That is why God promises to never leave us. It reminds us that we can be transparent and "let it all hang out" trusting that He will always be the ultimate covering.

As your friend, I am committed to showing you the worst of me and also telling you what God has done in my life. I'll let you know that it's okay if things suck. I won't ask you to put a mask over your pain. I will step into it with you. I will suffer with you and help carry your burden. Then together we'll experience the joy that's going to come in the morning. Because that is what God promises—joy will come in the morning. And on the days when it feels impossible to believe, remember that I am believing for you.

A word of caution. Once you embrace a transparent lifestyle, be prepared that it will not always be well received. Some might even question your level of faith. The truth is that as you start to embrace the freedom and joy that God has waiting for you, even in the midst of pain, there will be people who are (for lack of a better word) jealous of your joy. So let's agree now that when we are tempted to criticize someone else's level of faith, we will instead look for opportunities to share our own. When our faith is strong, we can intercede and step into the gap for someone who is struggling. Can we make a pact and agree on this?

Fear is a thorn in my side and a struggle that I have yet to fully escape. Because of that, activating my faith can be difficult. I am not afraid to let others know when my faith is weak. This conversation can make people who are inexperienced with open expressions of "weak" faith uncomfortable. That's okay. Sometimes, all you have is a mustard seed, and you know what? That's enough for God.

Remember, you don't have to try to build yourself up in the middle of the mess. God's going to do that work for you. You only have to make room for Him by getting all of the stuff out there and then letting it go. Free your hands up to receive what

He wants to give you. Once your hands are free, you can help the people that God puts in your path. God wants you to extend to others the same comfort He has given to you. That's the purpose.

Fear and judgment will creep in during the tough times and convince you that things will never be good again and that you are weak for feeling crappy. That just isn't true and it isn't biblical either! Those pesky voices still sneak up on me and attack my most vulnerable wounds! But I know that God's got me and that no matter how I am feeling, He is still a God that never fails. Maybe today you are feeling tired, defeated, and weak. It's okay. In the middle of the most challenging times, God is nurturing something in you and making room for spectacular blessings on the other side of the pain. God does not want you to settle for less! He wants you to prepare for more! He has already planned to exceed your expectations. Will you choose to believe?

> *God does not want you to settle for less!*

Make It Personal

Have you ever wanted to scream, "I'M NOT OKAY!" If so, you are in good company. Have you ever felt judged by others or yourself because your faith was weak our you anxiety was peaking?

Without judgment for yourself

I challenge you to do something strange—Are you with me? OK get alone in a place where you won't scare anyone and then think about a situation present or past when you really felt uncomfortable about admitting that you were struggling. Now, take a deep diaphragmatic breath and yell, "I'M NOT OK!...OK?!" Do it as many times as you need too. **Now check in with yourself.** How did that feel to make room for your truth?

What can you do **RIGHT NOW** to turn that statement into a prayer? I encourage you to do it. Let God know and ask Him to increase you faith and wipe out your fear.

"Hey, Grief! Let Me Introduce You to Hope!"

"Grief is never convenient, and we are not in control of its timeline. It chooses us; it is unavoidable, yet necessary, and everyone will experience it multiple times in their lives. To grow, we must get comfortable with grieving."

There are countless questions woven into grief's journey— the "what ifs," the "why me-s," the "what nows," and many other unformed groans that are impossible to verbally articulate, which nestle deeply into our souls. Grief needs space to breathe and time to transform. How much time? I don't know; no one does. Every person and every situation is different. Either way, we must give ourselves and the people we love enough space and grace to let these questions linger.

During the early years of marriage, Lenny and I faced hurdles that many couples don't have to tackle in a lifetime. The avalanche of crises that could have torn Lenny and me to pieces would prove to become the foundation for a resilient partnership. The difficulties would build us up, establish our love, and strengthen our faith. To *survive*, we needed to give up control, embrace the mess, and wade slowly through grief. To *thrive*, we had to embrace each other, choose hope, and cling to Jesus. Do you see the difference? Surviving is important, and it's the first step toward healing. But to make room for joy, we must figure out how to THRIVE.

By now, we have adequately determined that grief is a recurring theme in my life. Maybe it is for you too. I used to believe that this made me unique, that it was merely my cross to bear. But the more I share my story and listen to the stories of others, I have come to realize that grief is woven into everyone's journey. It is the major recurring theme in everyone's life. Grief unites us because we all have losses sometimes. Dreams are extinguished, failures happen, people die, marriages end, friendships dissolve, innocence is lost, and realities shift. Grief arrives in many different colors, forms, and experiences. Grief doesn't ask permission or wait for an invitation to show up. It ebbs and flows in and out of our lives at will. Sometimes it rushes in like a raging river that swells beyond its banks, flooding the landscape of our souls. Other times, it passes as quickly as it has appeared, like a brief summer's afternoon rain. And then, there are those times when grief relentlessly seeps and settles in every nook of our hearts. A sadness is consistently replenished from so many different angles because of years of crises that it feels impossible to address the root cause. Everything turns cold, damp, and gray, and finding a dry safe place to take refuge becomes difficult. How can anything thrive in this environment?

When God chose not to answer our prayers and breathe life into our whisper of hope, I felt betrayed. I felt like a fool. I was ashamed of the God that I served. I thought to myself, "What kind of testimony am I? How on earth can I sing in a choir and speak encouragement to others in need when bad things just keep happening to me?" I felt like a fraud. People saw me as an overcomer, but I was telling myself the opposite. I repeated words of destruction to myself: "You are not an overcomer, but a fake. You are useless and less than … God doesn't love you the way He loves other people." Anger, pain, and suffering rolled in and once again weighed heavily on my soul. The grief I was experiencing was complicated and hard to define. I was grieving physical things, spiritual things, and emotional things.

I felt like a disappointment to my husband, to a man who dreamt of having way too many children and had waited his whole life to get married. He prayed for a wife, and I am what he ended up with; what a disappointment. What did I have to offer him? I was always fatigued, and sex was complicated because of cancer, surgeries, and leftover emotional trauma. Now, my womanhood had been carved out of my body and discarded like trash—no breasts and no ovaries were present. I was also experiencing the full effects of menopause. The result: painful sex—both physically and emotionally. There was no joy or happiness attached to the idea of "trying to start a family" or using intimacy as a tool for comfort. The mere act of creating a child was tarnished, and I was hyper-aware that nothing happening in my bedroom was going to lead to a beautiful baby.

The feelings of rejection and the repetitive destructive mantra, "You're not good enough!" echoed loudly in the emptiness of my inner being and made plenty of room for fear to move in. I was isolated and alone. Honestly, I prayed that God would give me cancer again and let me die. Finally, there would be an exclamation point in my life. Then my husband could find another woman with good genetics and a non-hostile womb. He could have the wife and experiences that I was sure he longed for and that I was unable to provide.

Talking to me about anything became a lose-lose for Mr. Walker. The more he tried to encourage me, the angrier I became. I was inconsolable and not open to reason or possibility. It seemed like every day, something would happen to set me off. My mood could change rapidly from contentment to despair. I especially hated when people would ask about why we didn't have children, and I felt judged when onlookers were comfortable telling us that it was time for us to adopt. I still hate it. Do people honestly think that adoption is the best treatment plan for failed IVF and the gaping wound of infertility? When people— with their excellent intentions—tell a woman who has suffered the grief of a mis-carriage or a failed IVF that they can try again, sometimes they actually can't. Perhaps they can't afford it financially or they cannot afford it spiritually or mentally. Maybe they are exhausted from dreaming, only to be disappointed. For my husband and me, this was the only chance for us to have biological children that were part of me and part of him. As an adoptee, I had always dreamt of having a child that was the flesh of my flesh. Growing up, I was obsessed with family resemblances, and I longed to experience the reflection connection which proves to yourself and to the world that you belong somewhere—that you are a part of a tribe and that you have people who are intimately and genetically tied to you.

What a gift it is to be able to look into the eyes of a brother or sister, a mother or father, a cousin, uncle, or aunt and see bits of yourself staring back at you. You might see your beautiful smile or your perfectly sculpted cheekbones. Maybe you have your father's eyes, but your mother's legs, and this is not just something that *you* notice. Even the things that you dislike about yourself take on new meaning when you share those characteristics with a blood relative. Perhaps you have Auntie June's big nose or Uncle Jerry's hairy arms. These become constant visual reminders that you belong somewhere. There is a confidence that comes from knowing that you share something so unique and special with those people who are closest to you, your family.

For most of my life, I could only imagine how that felt, and I know that I am not alone. For many people, the gift of seeing the family around them hidden in their own reflection is a foreign experience. For many adoptees, it is a reality that lives only in our fantasies.

So, when people hear that you are barren and unable to have biological children, they often follow up with, "Well ... have you ever considered adoption? You should adopt—you're adopted, so it's the perfect thing for you to do." They're right; we can adopt, and quite honestly, it is one of the only options left for us. But adoption isn't a treatment plan for the grief that emerges from infertility. Adoption isn't the answer to the millions of questions that are embedded in its journey. That wound needs time to heal. **When you use adoption as an oversized bandage for infertility-induced grief, you never fully recover because the wounds continue to be susceptible to the stubborn infections of fear and doubt.**

So how do you experience love and wade through grief amidst this kind of pain? How do you thrive *through* grief? These are questions that both Mr. Walker and I have faced. There is nothing fun or sexy about tackling cancer or infertility as newlyweds. Instead of spending time embracing each other, you are forced to wrap your arms around pain. It is uncomfortable and exhausting. It's easy to look at pictures of Lenny and me and hear stories of how he cared for me when I had cancer and lifted me when we experienced miscarriage and assume that we are better at this relationship thing than other people. NOT TRUE—just ask Lenny.

The only thing that we might be better at is choosing to stay—even when it's uncomfortable. We choose to love when we don't feel like it, reflect when it doesn't come naturally, extend grace when we don't want to offer it, and accept each other when we know that failure is inevitable. It's an everyday thing. Relationships are hard when things are going well, so we shouldn't be surprised at the level of work it takes when grief and suffering have decided to move in! Part of working through grief is learning to prepare for it so that you can support each other during it and find your way back to hope when the landscape doesn't look familiar.

You must be prepared to fail each other along the way. There is an opportunity for overflowing beauty and joy when you embrace a grace-filled posture and journey through ALL of life with someone. We had to choose God first, especially on the days when it was impossible to choose each other. His love soothes, comforts, and heals. He gives us the strength needed to love through our own brokenness and bridge the gap for someone who is too exhausted to choose it for themselves.

This action plan can be applied to most relationships. Perhaps you are grieving with a friend, a parent, or a sibling? Maybe you are trying to figure out what to say to someone who has just lost a child or a relationship. Remember, their grief isn't a question that needs an answer! But your faith, hope, joy, and love can be shared. Let the act of choosing and sharing love fuel the joy that feelings of grief or pain have momentarily stolen!

Grief isn't a question that needs an answer!

Some months after we began to resurface from the devastation of miscarriage, a package arrived in the mail. It might have been addressed to both Mr. Walker and me, but I knew it was just for me because it was from our earth angel Deena—our gestational carrier. There is a special bond that forms between a woman who can carry a baby and offers up her womb and a woman who finds herself in need of such an offer. We will be connected for the rest of our lives in a way that is so intimate it is hard to describe. The box was filled to the brim with things she knew I would love, but there was one gift that I will treasure above all the others.

A simple buttercup yellow-hued book. This is a gift that would both torment me and transform me. It would become an essential highlight on my journey through the stages of grief. The pages were numerous. They were filled with promptings and spaces to document all of the moments of one's pregnancy, like what you were feeling during each trimester, pictures of sonograms, what kinds of weird cravings you were experiencing, the size of your belly—all sorts of tidbits and milestones. There were empty pages for recording memorable birth scenarios and everything that happened during those first few sleepless nights and months. Spaces were designated for fingerprints, locks of hair, and records of weight. All of the big and small details, each holding great significance, had a special place in this small yellow-hued book.

This book was sent with a beautiful letter, a letter that I hope to share someday because it's a letter that is worth sharing.

This letter reminded me that even in our grief when horrible things happen to us and the dreams that we believed were led by God are squashed—there is still joy. When we prayerfully plan our journey only to find that the bridge we thought was going to take us to the other side has been wiped away by some disaster or unforeseen circumstance—there is still a purpose. When we are standing on the cliff's edge and anger and sadness have separated us from our hope—there is always a path. An alternate route to a destination that will exceed our expectations has already been planned. It's just out of sight. This letter reminded me that even when we're dwelling in painful circumstances, God still has a masterful plan—a plan to take the complications and transform them into something more beautiful than we can imagine.

God had a plan for our surrogate, and that "God plan" was set into motion long before our paths crossed. God knew that she needed this crisis for her own growth. At that moment, our journeys collided, and the broken pieces that were in her heart and soul that could only be addressed through a complete dependency on God would rise to the surface. I can only ascertain that in His wisdom, God knew that although this journey would be incredibly difficult and painful, we'd both come out stronger on the other side. After being thrown into grief, we would take our brokenness and our specks of faith, come together, and go searching for the bridge of hope down the road, the bridge that we had to believe was there. Her letter reminded me that my ways are not God's ways.

I stared at the neatly folded letter for some time before getting the courage to open my heart to the words of a woman who both carried and lost my whisper of hope. It took even longer to crack open the cover of the book! When I finally did begin to leaf through the pages, there was a strange excitement. After each of my cancer diagnoses, I thought perhaps I'd never know what it was like to get that call when someone says, "You're pregnant!" I'd never get to experience that joy. But I did, and I had the memories to prove it. There are many men and women who never even get that call. Yet as I smiled and experienced the warm joy of this memory, I knew that each new page led me closer to the emptiness, which ultimately defined this book. For every page that was filled, there were more pages that were empty.

Blank pages took the place of overflowing joy. The emptiness was suffocating. Grief had blocked access to fresh air and made it impossible for pain to escape. There wasn't a place in this book to attach pictures of tear-stained faces or swollen eyes. There was no writing prompt for all of the anger I was fighting to contain. There wasn't room to talk about my marriage and how difficult it was to share this grief with someone who processes sadness and loss so differently. Or what it was like to have the pregnancy come to an end so early into the journey. The pages were just empty—void of words and stories. Loneliness rose from the emptiness. These pages were desperate for a word of hope, a story of joy, and a happy ending.

I'm actually the only person who has looked at that book. Even my husband and my closest friends, who I thought might want to look, haven't inquired. I used to be hurt by this fact, but now I realize that they too are deeply affected by the loss. Silence and space are things we often long for, but rarely feel comfortable with. The emptiness of these pages reminds anyone who views them that disappointment and suffering happen. None of us are immune, and we are not in control. These blank pages force you to hope for something that is not yet seen. That, my friends, is faith.

> *The emptiness of these pages reminds anyone who views them that disappointment and suffering happen.*

"What is faith? It is the confident assurance that something we want is going to happen. It is the certainty that what we **HOPE** for is waiting for us, even though we cannot see it up ahead" Hebrews 11:1 (TLB, emphasis added).

Coming face-to-face with the emptiness and isolation of grief has given me space and time to shift my perspective. This book— every page of it—has transformed from torment into a treasure because I have to wonder, how does God want to fill up those empty pages? Often the beginning of the best must be started with the reality of the worst. Sometimes we have to be emptied out of everything old so that we can be filled up with all things new!

> *Sometimes we have to be emptied out of everything old so that we can be filled up with all things new!*

The word of God is clear that in this life, you will experience trials. Yet God also promises to do something amazing with those difficulties—if we choose to hope and trust Him.

"I have told you these things so that in me you may have peace. In this world, you will have trouble. But take heart! I have overcome the world." (John 16:33)

Whether we share the same faith base or not, we can all admit that at some point, everyone will lose something that devastates them. It's In the middle of the devastation that you must either choose hope or cozy up to the alluring state of hopelessness and shrink away. I decide to place my hope in God. A God that can do the impossible and promises to never leave me disappointed. A God who has kept me in the middle of the strongest storms. A God whose love can be trusted. If you choose the path of hope, then be prepared, because joy and peace are its results! The sorrow and grief don't evaporate—they're still there, and it's still hard. But somehow, the sadness becomes linked with joy and peace. Their coexistence sets the stage for transformation and gives you the courage to face the trials of each day. You begin to wait expectantly because you believe that God will take the complicated stuff and turn it into something beautiful.

> "We can rejoice, too, when we run into problems and trials, for we know that they help us develop endurance. And endurance develops strength of character, and character strengthens our confident hope of salvation. And this hope will not lead to disappointment. For we know how dearly God loves us."
>
> Romans 5:3-5

I will always treasure the first few pages of that yellow-hued book that chronicle the joy of our journey before the bridge was wiped away. Those are my pages; that is my story. I will also choose to believe that God is writing a new story that will fill every empty space and use my pain to fuel my purpose. I will open that book, cross out the old headings, and create new ones for myself. I will clear space to talk about the tough stuff, be intentional about gratitude, and make room for joy. God is not finished with me yet. My story is not over, and neither is yours. What do your pages look like?

Has something been stolen from you? Has loss created an emptiness that seems impossible to fill? Does your hope seem to be trapped on the other side of a ravine—totally out of reach? I've been there. Taking the risk of faith is rarely easy or comfortable, but it's worth it. The benefit of choosing faith will always outweigh the risk of the initially uncertain outcome.

Taking the risk of faith is rarely easy or comfortable, but it's worth it.

Do you want your faith to be so great that there isn't any room left for fear? I sure do.

I want to choose to hope in the things that I cannot see—because that is where faith lives. When your faith is alive, you can thrive! Don't trust me. Trust God, introduce your grief to hope, and then take a leap of faith to claim the joy God has for you. I promise you, it will be worth it.

Make It Personal

How is your relationship with hope today? Are you struggling? Is it strong in one area but weak in another? That's okay! And completely normal.

Without judgment for yourself

I challenge you to meditate on where you might need to reintroduce hope into your life. What would it feel like if HOPE was permanently engraved on your dance card? Write it down or speak it out loud! Cry out in prayer and let God take the weight of loss and disappointment and clothe you in peace and joy! **Now check in with yourself.** What insight have you gained?

What can you do **RIGHT NOW** to reintroduce hope into you daily regime?

Part 5

Make Room for Joy

Pain, Power, and Possibilities

"Growth requires you to embrace the problems by leaning into the possibilities!"

Have you ever noticed that after enduring a crisis, you miraculously transform into a skilled encourager?

Someone hears your story and ends up being inspired and encouraged because of your suffering, pain, or failure. If this sounds familiar, then you have experienced the point and the purpose behind the tough times. The power of your story isn't in the laundry list of practical advice you can give someone, but rather the love, compassion, and hope you can generously share with the world because you have spent some time walking the pathways of adversity.

The more possibilities you see amidst your pain, the more joy and contentment there is available for you and for others. Your story's power multiplies when you connect it to God. I forgot this vital truth not too long ago. I had finally committed to writing this book, and in full transparency, I was in total fear mode. I have always been good at encouraging others; definitely one of my gifts, but encouraging myself? Not so much. I am an expert at trusting in other people's abilities, giftings, and callings, but I struggle with believing in my own. The never-ending quest for belonging and my desperate need to feel useful have impacted my identity significantly.

I was reminded of this during one of my weekly therapy appointments. After listening intently to me recount my thoughts, fears, and anxieties from the past week, my therapist paused and then said, "It seems to me that you might have a problem with trust. Not trust in God, but trust in yourself." I spent some time thinking about this after our session, and I realized that I had stopped trusting who God created me to be. I'd discontinued having faith in my ability to make an impact. I was letting the fear of failure creep in and momentarily fracture my story's connection to God's truth. My identity could not be rooted in both fear and the things of God. I had to make a choice—and so do you. When we believe that we are who God says we are, we have the freedom to shake off our fear, trust ourselves, and see the opportunity for joy in every circumstance.

> *My identity could not be rooted in both fear and the things of God.*

I was having a hard time grasping on to joy and peace, and I was making the lives around me—especially Mr. Walker's—miserable. I don't know how he puts up with me! At this time, I'd disconnected from my light source and I was choosing to lay down in the darkness and wallow. I could see everyone else's light, but not my own. My light wasn't stolen. I simply chose to turn it off and set up camp in the deep, dark valley of victimhood. Fear makes it easy to forget that we have a choice when it comes to how we interact with crisis and how we choose to embrace our value and identity. It takes courage and boldness to step out in faith and be all that God has equipped us to be.

God wants our difficulties to activate our purpose, not persuade us into a passive, pessimistic routine. To choose the path of possibility, you must trust who God says you are. You must decide to switch on your own light, the light that is powered by love, hope, and faith. The God who created the heavens and the earth and every living thing wants you and me to be the hands and feet of sacrificial service and love that this world needs. Are you ready? Isn't it amazing that He has given us such an important calling? We were fashioned and created to play specific and essential roles to impact our world for good. God wants us to think big—really big.

That day in my therapist's office, my recurring momentary amnesia took control of my mind and heart. I forgot the point and purpose behind everything I'd endured. I didn't trust my ability to have an impact. Why should I tell my story? What did I really have to offer? These questions were racing through my mind. My Intense anxiety and irrational thoughts were masking the truth of who I'd become because of my crises. My therapist's observations and my continued reflection reminded me that to thrive, I had to choose to be the light in the middle of my own darkness. I had to choose to believe that I was fearfully and wonderfully made and that God had a plan to prosper me, lead me, love me, comfort me, catch me, and use me. God has equipped me and prepared me to have an impact, one which will continue to exceed my expectations. But to make it happen, I have to step out in faith and activate my trust in God and myself.

There are times in life when it feels impossible to see God reflected in the mirror. I struggle with low self-esteem, poor body image, self-doubt, and significant anxiety. I routinely avoid my own reflection because I don't trust that I will love what I see. I have a hard time looking past my own judgment and negative self-talk to see who I really am. I forget that God made me exactly how He wanted me to be created. It can be hard to truly love others when you loathe yourself. A big part of stepping into God's purpose is embracing the you that God sees, the you that He created perfectly and in His image. For many of us, this is a lifelong struggle. But it is imperative to tackle this demon if we are to truly understand the point of life and step into joy, possibility, and purpose.

My second mom, Elsie, has lived her whole life seeking after the kingdom of God and working toward loving and trusting herself. Her life's purpose was established and solidified because of her trials and tribulations. My mom's voice was stolen from her early on in life and for many years, she didn't have the strength or courage to search for that missing voice. Her lack of courage was not an indication of cowardice, but instead a result of suffering years of rejection and oppression. She was convinced that quiet and passive were better than fierce and opinionated. She forgot that her faith made her more than a conqueror. There was no one to advocate for her when she needed it most, and she had not been empowered to advocate for herself. The mental illness, infertility, and low self-esteem that attached themselves to her early on were considered blemishes—things to hide and be ashamed of. She was told what to do and how to act. The childhood descriptors of being unimportant and not worthy followed after her into adulthood. There wasn't much room for her to grow or dream.

My mom, Mama Elsie, is the ultimate giver. I have watched her give tirelessly to everyone until there was nothing left for her to give back to herself. Early on, this

> *A lack of courage was not an indication of cowardice.*

influence cultivated the belief in me that to consider oneself is a selfish act. I believed that there was nothing admirable about taking care of yourself or speaking words of affirmation or praise about yourself. I've never heard my mom compliment herself. She has never said (to me) about herself: I am beautiful. I am smart. I am worthy.

Yet even with these complexities, my mom continues to be the most inspirational influence in my life. To some, she might appear to be overly sensitive, flighty, and maybe even fragile, but what I see is a woman who is fierce and mighty because her strength is drawn directly from the all-powerful God. Embedded in her weakness, there has always been a God-infused core of steel. She possesses a strength and resilience that is impossible to describe. My mom doesn't waste time trying to figure out every "why" or understand every trial. She sees the possibilities for service, generosity, and compassion that are sprinkled throughout every day—and she acts on them! She brings warmth to the coldest, most dreary moments, and refreshment to those unbearably hot ones. Her presence is always a blessing.

The truth is my mom never taught me how to speak words of goodness over my own being. I routinely struggle with seeing my own value. Self-deprecation comes so naturally to me that it is difficult for me to embrace encouragement, compliments, and love. I have trouble believing that anyone could find me attractive or beautiful or that I am worthy of being treasured and cherished. These struggles are ongoing. Thankfully, through my mom, I have also discovered how important it is to strive after God's love so that HE can help me see how beautiful and worthy I truly am. My mom also reminds me that it's okay to struggle. It's okay to not be okay; it's natural and doesn't alter your potential impact and purpose.

My mom hates getting her picture taken, and so do I. The rise of social media and cell phones that are equipped to capture every visual moment is overwhelming. I am hypercritical of each picture that is taken of me and feel like I will never really have that perfect, Instagram-worthy face, body, or smile. I am that woman who puts makeup on before going to the gym and reapplies foundation at the beach! I look and feel my best with concealer, mascara, and bronzer, and I'm okay with that.

Growing up, I was jealous of the girls who could jump in a pool without reservation and look just as good, if not better when they emerged. For years, I convinced myself that women with flawless skin and no cellulite were somehow prettier, smarter, more capable, and easier to love than me. The struggle to accept yourself fully, from the inside out, is a journey that doesn't come naturally to many of us.

Finally, at age forty-something, I am starting (just starting) to embrace a different perspective. But this is not easy. The constant picture taking forces me to "face" myself regularly, and I am not always thrilled about what I see. I easily observe the effects of chemotherapy, surgeries, menopause, and grief. Drug-induced fatigue taints my skin and highlights the bags under my eyes. Do I think that I am beautiful? Yes, sometimes—but it's hard work.

A few years ago, the news anchors on my favorite morning television show went makeup-free for a day. They all took turns critiquing their barefaced selves in a hall of mirrors. As I watched, I began thinking about my own reflection. I remembered moments staring back at myself, sometimes with a giant smile, but often with tears streaming down my face. Ten years ago, after my first cancer diagnosis, I was forced into an encounter with a new reflection, and it wasn't love at first sight!

Remember my friend who took me to the fancy New York City salon to have my hair cut off during chemo? Well, I never wanted short hair, and that day I was more interested in mourning my beauty than believing that true beauty resided far beneath my luxurious locks. As I left the salon, I didn't recognize the girl staring back at me in the windows of the fancy Fifth Avenue stores. Every stranger I passed on the congested New York City streets seemed to be staring at me. Could they see the pain I was carrying around with me? Could they tell I was terrified? It was like someone had turned my body inside out, exposing my wounded, fear-filled soul for the whole world to see. A season of suffering was upon me. I was angry, afraid, and sad.

Yet, somewhere piled beneath the crisis, there was a spark of hope. I am pretty confident that was God whispering, "You are beautiful. You can do this. Trust me. Have faith. You are stronger than you think. Remember, you are more than a conqueror!" From that moment on, I would never look at myself in the same way because scars and pain are now a permanent part of my reflection.

"You are beautiful. You can do this. Trust me. Have faith. You are stronger than you think. Remember, you are more than a conqueror!"

Becoming acquainted and comfortable with my reflection after this crisis would take some serious work! At first, I could only handle short glimpses because I couldn't embrace words of care, kindness, and acceptance. Cancer forced my scars to rise to the surface, and it's easy for me to name this as the primary source for my lack of self-love, but truthfully, I never liked my reflection.

We all face insecurities as children. I grew up feeling less than and often forgotten. This pain was birthed out of a fear of rejection and the unnamed loss rooted in my adoption. I'd also been betrayed, mocked, and belittled in the most intimate relationships.

I'd watched all the men in my life choose themselves over the women who loved them. Toxic fumes filled up my inner being. I needed a spiritual cleansing that required me to consciously breathe in the truth of who God said I was and breathe out the lies that had filled my soul for too long. Slowly, ever so slowly, I began to see past the scars and love the woman who was emerging from beneath the rubble of crisis. She was perfectly imperfect, totally complicated, surprisingly resilient, and equipped to make a significant impact in this world.

At some point, I had to decide that it wasn't necessary to understand everything to move past the pain and step into my purpose. To grow, I had to get comfortable with being still. I needed to cast my gaze on the unseen things, instead of every complicated circumstance. I had to lean into Jesus, instead of leaning into fear. To make room for joy, I needed to also make room for grief, suffering, and uncertainty. I needed to be okay with letting my pain sit close to the surface because God wanted me to use that pain to help others. I had to slow down, take a breath, and really soak in every moment because gratitude was necessary to survive and only possible if I made time for it. I had to shift my perspective on crisis and begin to embrace the beauty of each complicated moment. To thrive, I had to believe that a new joy was possible every single day.

Six years ago, I stood again naked in front of the mirror. Scattered across my body was a visual roadmap of crises. The scars on my breasts were more visible than those that were now present on my abdomen; these were small, exact, and almost undetectable in the flattering evening light. Even still, I knew they were there. I was grateful to be alive, but I was also totally devastated because this roadmap led to a barren destination. As my gaze rested intently on my midsection, I was reminded that just a month prior, the powers of reproduction still existed. I was now fully clothed in the realities and repercussions of multiple cancers. I would never see a baby bump in my reflection or celebrate through pictures and personal memories the miraculous gift of carrying my own child. That would not be a part of my journey.

Strangely, that night I felt more beautiful than I had in a long time. For years, I complained about my body, expressing freely all of the things that I wasn't satisfied with. But at that moment, I wanted everything to stay the same. After a lifetime of wishing for smaller thighs, less cellulite, and clearer skin, I was finally grateful for the body that I did have. I was alive. The next morning, I would head to the hospital to have double mastectomies, and once again, I would be forced to get acquainted with a new reflection.

Does this resonate with you? When you catch a glimpse of yourself, are you pleased with what you see? Do the complications embedded in your reflection build you up or tear you down? Are you filled with love and gratitude or criticism and regret? Do you see pain, hurt, or loss reflected? Do you speak and accept words of affirmation or let the criticism and crises of the past contaminate your soul? Do you trust that God has a purpose for your pain—all of it? Now is the time to take a long look in the mirror, choose hope, and speak life into your reflection—say it: **"I am beautiful. I am fearfully and wonderfully made. I am more than a conqueror, and God has plans—many plans—to prosper me and use me."** As hard as it might be to do this, I promise it is the right decision—because the alternative to speaking life is death. If we are not growing from our grief, pain, and disappointments, then we are dying from them.

> *Now is the time to take a long look in the mirror, choose hope, and speak life into your reflection.*

> *"He cuts off every branch in me that bears no fruit, while every branch that does bear fruit he prunes so that it will be even more fruitful."*
> John 15:2 (NIV)

Letting go is painful! I've had to let go of a lot of things in my life—loved ones, marriages, dreams, friends, and even body parts. Things literally had to be cut away

> *If we are not growing from our grief, pain, and disappointments, then we are dying from them.*

from me so that I could live! The journey from grief to growth takes TIME. It requires care, patience, faith, and perseverance. It's messy, complicated, and painful. And that's okay. Pain is the pathway to purpose. When you operate in a place of hope and gratitude, pain miraculously transforms into a powerful, strength-infused glow.

> *The journey from grief to growth takes TIME.*

Visible scars are softened by a beautiful resilience that a crisis cannot erase. Joy is easier to cultivate when you are fixed on the possibilities, not just the problems. To do this, you must turn away from hopelessness, even when it is beckoning you with vats of sinfully delicious ice cream and hours of mindless binge-watching!

> *Joy is easier to cultivate when you are fixed on the possibilities, not just the problems.*

Choosing hope and seeking joy amidst a crisis is not a passive pastime, but active, firm, and relentless. You begin by confronting the negative voices and standing up to them with the power of gratitude and self-love. You must remind yourself that you are who God says you are.

When you lean into Christ, you have access to the power of the resurrection and to the power that raises the dead, heals the sick, and parts the seas. You are loved, beautiful, strong, and powerful because you are a child of God. Your complications are beautiful because God created you and He does all things well. You are more than a conqueror and you have a purpose! When you match the onslaught of negative voices with God's truths, you can expect victory; suffering does not miraculously disappear in the presence of hope, but how you interact with pain is altered significantly and this transforms everything.

> *You are loved, beautiful, strong, and powerful because you are a child of God.*

Today, when I look in the mirror, I encounter a beautiful, resilient woman of faith—not just a survivor, but a thriver! I still don't like my thighs, and I don't plan on actively participating in "No Makeup Mondays" or "Forget Your Spanx Sundays," so please don't ask! Every moment, I will fight to get up, step out of despair, and jump into joy, whether I am feeling it or not. Sometimes the choice will be easy, and other times, it will feel impossible, but I will do it anyway because the results of choosing HOPE will always be joy-filled! Are you with me?

My mom may not have taught me how to love my reflection, but she did teach me how to love God. She has taught me to love without borders and see God in the worst of circumstances. Through her actions, I have learned that it is better to get up than to stay down. When we reach out to God and let Him be the steady hand which pulls us up, we are bound to live a life full of purpose (even if we don't always see it—or feel it).

God wants to use us in ways that we cannot imagine. When life sucks, you must choose to get up, face forward, and insist that God do something with the mess. He is looking for people to be His hands extended, and the suffering you've endured equips you to give back.

> *When life sucks, you must choose to get up, face forward, and insist that God do something with the mess.*

I doubt there will ever be a time when it is easy for my mom to shower herself with compliments. So I will continue to tell her what she says to me, "You are beautiful. You are strong. You are smart. You are kind. You are worthy. You are loved." My mom's generous spirit and active giving have made an impact on this world that is equal to kings, queens, and Nobel Peace Prize winners. When she leaves this earth, her name might not be remembered by many, but be assured she is one famous celebrity in the place that she is headed. Heaven definitely knows my mom's name.

God prepared my mom for parenthood by allowing her to struggle through some unthinkable situations. She didn't need parenting classes to care for me. Her trials were the training that was required to support and comfort me during my lifetime of difficulties. God comforts you during your troubles so that you can comfort others in theirs. Not a similar comfort, not

> *God comforts you during your troubles so that you can comfort others in theirs.*

an adequate comfort, but the same comfort that God has given you. Now that is a superpower that I want to have access to!

> *"He comforts us in all our troubles so that we can comfort others. When they are troubled, we will be able to give them the same comfort God has given us."*
>
> *2 Corinthians 1:4*

Comfort comes in different sizes and styles. Sometimes comfort is sturdy, like tough love. Sometimes comfort is soft and gentle, like a soothing voice in the middle of a loud and chaotic environment. And sometimes, it is the voice of reason when irrational thoughts have invaded your mental territory. See, even comfort is complicated!

Whatever crisis you have endured or are enduring, God has given you the power to take His comfort and offer it to someone else. Suffering is never easy, but do not assume that beauty cannot be found amidst it. There is nothing more beautiful than making an eternal impact on the world around you. God uses the cycle of comfort to change people's lives.

Are you suffering from the growing pains of grief or disappointment? I encourage you to choose hope. Have faith, because the master gardener is doing a mighty work in you. He is doing what is needed so that you can grow to greater heights! God's plans and dreams for YOU are more than you could ever imagine! Let Him comfort, guide, and nurture you during these times so that you will become fully established, faith-filled, and joy*full*.

When you believe that there are possibilities and purpose in every circumstance and that God will use your complicated situation to bring comfort through you to others, the less shocked and disoriented you'll be when adversity hits. When you place your hope in a God that promises to keep you, protect you, and defend you—you don't have to fear failure or difficulties. The more you lean into God, the easier it is to lean away from fear and doubt. The more we trust what God promises to do with our troubles, the easier it will be to choose hope and experience joy.

I did not enjoy having cancer, nor did I enjoy being told I would never bear children. No one enjoys those things, but what I did cherish was being cared for by others, especially Mr. Walker. It was beautiful, and I would've never experienced that if it had not been for the complications of cancer.

Remember, it's not just about you. It's about the people who surround you. My husband learned to pray by praying for me. He learned to encourage by encouraging and cook by cooking! Lenny learned so much by actually doing things. My pain provided an opportunity for his personal growth. God used our crises to help us build a firm partnership—one that is now established and can withstand the onslaught of tidal waves that life might bring. Our relationship is more durable and our bond tighter because of cancer, infertility, and pain. What could have torn us apart wove us closer together. Now that is a beautiful thing!

Remember the young lady I mentioned earlier, who was in the middle of a marital crisis and new in the choir, the same choir I had joined during a similar time in my life? My experiences and the comfort God provided to me during my own struggles enabled me to speak life into this young woman. Not because I was a skilled coach or an inspirational influencer, but because I had been there. I too, had stood in the middle of betrayal, desperate for supernatural comfort.

My suffering equipped me to encourage her. God works in mysterious ways. You don't know how God wants to use your experience as an instrument of lifesaving change for someone else. And you won't ever find out unless you allow God the opportunity to work through you each day. The joy that inhabits you as a result of having come through the fire will be used to help others if you are open to the possibility.

Happiness is a good thing, but it's usually just for you. Joy is for everyone. We are inundated these days with talk about self-care, and it's easy to get stuck in the "self" part of self-care and self-love. We forget that our ultimate purpose lies outside of the inner circle, which consists of me, myself, and I. The purpose of our trials is so that we can bless, encourage, and serve others, not so that we can revel selfishly in our own contentment. People everywhere are desperate to feel and know that they matter. They want to be seen, acknowledged, validated, and valued. Isn't that what we all want? God fills us up and enlarges our territory so that we can have an enormous impact on the world.

The joy that inhabits you as a result of having come through the fire will be used to help others if you are open to the possibility.

Do you desire to have a significant impact and experience all of God's blessings? Then you must shift your perspective away from your inner circle and start seeing self-care as only the first step toward a life saturated in compassionate service. God created us to be givers. Service fuels joy. Ask yourself the questions: What now, God? How do you want to use this to help someone else? Then your joy is activated because it truly is better to give than to receive. Generosity is the key to living an abundant and purposeful life. The more you have endured and the more things you have survived and experienced, the more you have to give. What would it be like if we could see every trial as a gift and an opportunity for joy? How would that one shift totally change our lives and the lives of everyone we connect with? Think about the faith-fueled ripple effect of joy that we'd release. Imagine if everyone that met us left our presence a more hope-filled, joyful person.

Generosity is the key to living an abundant and purposeful life.

It's hard to be generous when you are discontented continuously, jealous, and feeling beat down. And it's impossible to be generous when hopelessness is your go-to tactic for crisis management. Generosity cannot exist when self-care has transformed into selfishness and, in many cases, narcissism. Real, sustainable, and ever-present, life-altering peace and joy are impossible when generosity is absent. To let the purpose of pain blossom, you must be generous with yourself and your joy.

This life is a series of races, road trips, and detours that never stop. Whatever part of the journey you're in at this moment, God has it in His view. Every moment, whether pleasant or painful, has a purpose. That is the miraculous result of granting God an all-access pass to your life. To help others, you have to show them the truth. You have to let your life be seen in an honest light, not the glossy magazine version. Be real with people and commit to removing the romanticism from the journey of pain and suffering.

Remember the story of Joseph and the coat of many colors? All kinds of bad stuff happened to him, but God had a plan in play that was going to blow his mind AND change the lives of many people.

[Joseph said] Don't you see, you planned evil against me, but God used those same plans for my good, as you see all around you right now—life for many people. (Genesis 50:20)

Just like Joseph, God wants to use every part of our journey to bring joy and hope to the world. When you choose hope and transparently share your story, observers will quickly see what really sustained you during the most challenging moments of life. The peace you embody during the storms of life is a beacon of hope for those who are searching. Everyone wants more peace and joy.

Sharing your joy in the middle of suffering lets others know that they have the power to activate theirs too. When you share authentically, you will encourage others to do the same. Your light will serve as a reminder to people that they also can shine in the middle of the darkness. The world doesn't need more inspirational quotes, journals, and motivational conferences to tell us to keep going. The world needs more generous people to share their light and their joy. Choose to keep your story connected to God and just watch Him exceed your expectations.

"Let us think of ways to motivate one another to acts of love and good works."
Hebrews 10:24 (NLT)

Joyful, love-filled people are motivated and equipped to do good things! It's easy to get fixated on how everything around us is affecting our own joy and productivity. But how often do we consider how we are harming the joy quotient and the richness of the people we rub shoulders with each day? How can we change our own attitudes to help promote love, productivity, and good works in the people we love, lead, and serve?

When you are tapped into joy and anchored to the faith, you are poised to spread goodness wherever you go! After all, what is the point of JOY? Is it to be hoarded, protected, and kept only for ourselves? Or is its purpose to soothe and refresh our souls with the expectation that we will then actively give joy back to the world around us. Struggles and pain don't steal joy. Instead, they intensify joy.

The greatest joy I have experienced has come when I am sharing my struggles with others who are in need. My own weakness and grief have prepared me

> *Struggles and pain don't steal joy. Instead, they intensify joy.*

to approach the pain of others with greater understanding and empathy. In this act of sharing and giving, joy miraculously multiplies.

Remember, crisis, pain, and grief are not things that we can avoid in this life. So instead of trying to run away from them, I say, "Embrace them!" Look them straight in the eye, stand your ground, and take from them all that you can. Let the sorrow you feel for a night transform into JOY in the morning. Then share it with someone! Good feelings and contentment that are kept only for oneself are not JOY. The fullness of JOY comes not only from embracing the crisis, but also from practicing the presence of God. Arm yourself with faith so that you can embrace difficulties, choose hope, and open the doors of your soul to JOY. It is not always easy—but easy is overrated. The JOY journey is worth sacrificing temporary ease for something greater and more fulfilling. When you are full and overflowing, you have enough to give and share. As you engage in this action and as you spread your joy, your cup will always be full. **I promise!**

Make It Personal

What would it be like if we could see every trial as a gift and an opportunity for joy? How would that one shift totally change our lives and the lives of everyone we connect with?

Without judgment for yourself

I challenge you to get real about you joy quotient today! What still needs to be removed from the table to make room for joy? **Now check in with yourself.** Take a moment and imagine what it would feel like to embody an indestructible, God-powered joy all of the time! This is possible—say it out loud, "It is possible for me to experience joy in the middle of the mess! My JOY will intensify because of my suffering and it will be easy to share and continuously overflowing."

What can you do **RIGHT NOW** to make room for more JOY and make space to share it with the world?

Read This Last. Please

I'm so glad that you made it to the end! You are still here! Thank you for showing up and taking this journey with me. Thank you for saying "Yes!" to more joy. Thank you for hearing me out and letting me challenge your perspectives on adversity, faith, hope, and perhaps a variety of other things. I am so grateful because your choices to embrace adversity differently, choose hope, and make room for joy will undoubtedly have a tremendous eternal impact on the world. Telling your story and sharing your truth with transparency will not always be easy. In fact, it will often be quite tricky. It takes courage to keep your pain close enough to the surface that you can easily access what is needed to encourage and speak life into someone who is in the midst of a crisis.

Sometimes God purposefully leads us into a place that is tight and uncomfortable. A place where we "feel" trapped. BUT if God has asked you to step out in faith and step into (or stay in) an unbearable situation, vocation, dream, ministry, leadership opportunity—whatever—then He is promising to be there with you. And with God, you will have access to a power that is proven to calm the violent seas and breathe life into death. God will lead you each step of the way, but only with enough guidance to get to the next step! The Lord's prayer says, "Give us this day our daily bread." It doesn't say, "Load us up for the week!" He doesn't want us to try and do what we don't know. He wants us to have faith and keep our eyes focused upward. It requires an act of faith to choose to believe that joy is possible when life feels impossible. Don't be distracted by what's happening in the periphery. He wants us to have so much faith in His ability to succeed that we can always operate in a place of hope and courage! It doesn't matter that you are stepping into a situation that seems to have no logical path to success, because you know a God who makes all things possible.

God is not practical but is instead all-powerful! It's in the place of uncertainty, at the bottom of the mountain, wedged between a rock and a hard place, that you must be bold and courageous, trusting that God will lead you to rest and satisfaction. We are not only to survive this life but to thrive, and with a sprinkle faith and a heavy dose of hope and gratitude, this is an achievable goal.

Life isn't easy, because it wasn't meant to be. It was designed to be complicated, just like us. And I don't want to leave you believing that by choosing to hope, you will miraculously experience joy and feel less pain. That is simply not true. Suffering stinks; it's miserable, it's dark, and it's depressing. It is going to be hard. But it doesn't have to prevent you from having a purpose. Pain doesn't need to derail your dreams because if given the opportunity, it promises to reshape your desires, strengthen your character, and establish your faith so that you can live out your dreams with joy! There will be plenty of days when pulling the covers over your head will be necessary—just do it and give yourself a break. **Remember it's okay not to be okay.** But please, don't set up camp there! Prepare for a crisis by deciding ahead of time that when the tsunami hits, you will choose to look up, choose hope, and seek help from God AND the people around you. And then take it one **beautifully complicated** moment at a time. Practice gratitude when it feels impossible. Stop and smell the roses, the bacon, your sweet child's hair, or the freshly cut grass. Making space to treasure life's simplest pleasures is guaranteed to increase your joy quotient and help you embrace every moment.

> *God is not practical but is instead all-powerful!*

You are a warrior and a victor, but you won't always feel this way. I routinely feel more like a worrier than a warrior. But the way I feel doesn't make it true! Disappointments, fatigue, failures, and sadness can quickly morph into worry and anxiety before you have a chance to resist them. They are like those mean girls (or boys) from high school who seem to know your weak spots. They observe and wait for the perfect time to disrupt your purpose and sabotage your joy with the weapons of lies and discouragement. So, when you come face to face with fear or worry, get real about how you are feeling and then take a moment to remind yourself who God says you are.

He says that you are MORE than a conqueror. He has given you access to a peace that surpasses understanding and a shield of faith that is equipped to defend anything that might come your way. So step into the victory that God has for you and leave the worry behind!

> *"No, in all these things (trouble, hardship, and persecution), we are more than conquerors through him who loved us."*
> *Romans 8:37*

My hope is that if you began this book as an unbeliever, you would finish it believing in God. This is the most significant decision you will ever make. And if doubt, pain, or suffering has stolen your belief, then I pray you will choose to believe again; remember that you are loved by God. He gave everything as a ransom for you, and He is waiting to welcome you back.

I hope that you find yourself empowered to rejoice in every crisis because you know God has great plans for you. And then, I hope you will keep believing, no matter what. Don't stop believing because of cancer, low self-esteem, betrayal, pain, failure, or disappointment. Don't stop believing because you don't feel like it anymore. Our hearts are deceptive, but God's power is not contingent upon how we feel.

God wants to do something new! He wants to use your grief, your sadness, your trials, and your difficulties for greatness. God wants you to lay your heavy burdens in His arms and take a long nap in the cashmere-lined pocket of peace that He's expertly knit into every circumstance.

It's hard to articulate my faith because it's greater than my mind can perceive. The only real formula for my "success" is Jesus. He is the lifter of my head, my constant comforter, and the source of my joy. Even when I am discouraged and question, "God, what next? What do you have for me?" or when I find myself battling with anxiety or afraid that I might never have children or that no one will read this book—God quietly speaks, "It's okay, I got you. I'm in the lead. Follow me because I am making a way and preparing to exceed your expectations. Will you trust me?"

I don't want my life to be defined by timelines, details, and diagnoses. I want my life to be defined by the joy I have experienced between the lines of every story that is written about me. That's what I want for you too. **This book is about YOU**, and I don't ever want you to feel like hopelessness is the only option because hope is the first step toward cultivating joy. I want you to experience a joy so great that it will be impossible to contain and easy to share. When you are tapped into joy and anchored to faith, you are poised to spread goodness everywhere you go!

I want you to experience a joy so great that it will be impossible to contain and easy to share.

Do you want to have an impact today? Then take some time to get real about the tough stuff so that you can make room for joy. And please share your story! Be real. Tell the truth. Let it be messy and complicated. Don't romanticize the moments that feel impossible, but share with the intention to help, to encourage, and to lift up!

Yes, life is hard, but it doesn't have to be void of joy, hope, and peace! (I'd like to think there is also room for beautiful views, bubble baths, and plenty of carbs too!)

When the voices of doubt, accusation, and fear are deafening you, choose to replace them with what you know to be true!

Now, repeat after me (I need to say them too!):

I am a Child of God who is fearfully and wonderfully made.
I am strong and I am kind.
I am the light in the darkest tunnel.
I am the voice of encouragement in the face of great suffering.
When I feel weak and uncertain, I still choose to grasp on to hope.
I can experience joy in the midst of a crisis.
I can do all that God has put before me.
I've got this because God's got ME!

Can I just say—one more time, "I am so glad that we are friends?" Friends share things, so I am leaving you with this prayer from my journal—please steal it, use it, and wear it out!

Dear God,

Grant me peace. Let me flee from anxiety, flee from fear, and flee from the one who wants to steal my purpose and sabotage my joy.

I believe that you see and know all things. God, you have already considered what I will eat, drink, and wear. My comings and goings are in focus and secured on the path you have created.

Your plan is perfect and without fault. Your timing is impeccable. God, your love is like a tidal wave—washing away my fear and clearing the crevices of my soul and mind that get crowded with the weight of the world. Thank you.

I hear you calling, "Return to me. Rest here." Help me to respond to this invitation and find comfort in the safety of your grace.

Then, please, God, use me. Use my story—every part of it. Use my joy and my sorrow.

Let me focus on your greatness and your love, so praise is forever on my lips and gratitude is always in my heart. Let those that I encounter have the desire to know more about the strength that resides in the core of my being—the power that is YOU.

Help me to be calm in the midst of chaos. Help me to bring joy where there is sorrow. Help me to show love in the face of hate. Help me to be an ambassador of peace to the discord which engulfs our world. You, Lord, are the answer. You were the answer yesterday, and You are the answer today. You know what is really amazing? You will be the answer tomorrow, too.

Oh ... and please don't forget to always exceed my expectations! You are the best! Amen.

With Gratitude

God has consistently placed people in proximity to my crisis, people who have helped to lift, lead, comfort, and sustain me during my most desperate times.

First, this book could never have been written without the encouragement and prodding from my friend and coach Liza. When I started working with her, I was afraid to write an Instagram caption , much less a book. I am incredibly grateful for her continued support and her unique ability to encourage and challenge me, always. She is a gift to this world.

By this point, it should go without saying that I am grateful to God, but I do have indescribable gratitude for the hand of God in my life. I continue to thrive because of Him and who He puts into my life. I am especially thankful for how He orchestrated the beginning of this journey through an impromptu New Year's Day girl's brunch at my friend Holly's house. It was that afternoon that I shared my desire to write a book, and she jumped at the chance to help by introducing me to the team at On Fire Books. It is there that I would meet Tammy, Patti, and Tiarra. They would encourage me to tell my story transparently and with the intention to help others transform their own lives. Tiarra spent many hours interviewing me and transcribing our calls so that I could figure out just how to tell my story. She helped make the daunting undertaking of writing a book feel manageable. She edited, reviewed, and edited and reviewed some more. She never said no to any request and her fingerprints are on every page. I will be forever grateful for her contribution. I must also thank Larry, Lori, and the whole team at Carpenter Son's Publishing. Having you on my team made so much more room for JOY.

I am also grateful for years of encouragement that I have received from my friends Catherine, Deionna, Barb, and Keisha. They have each taken time to critique and review words in the most practical ways. But their true contributions cannot be easily quantified. Catherine has taught me to tell my story by always applying her curiosity to our "talks." She is a masterful interviewer and an incredible friend. Deionna has taught me to embrace my creativity and live outside of the box that feels safe. She is the ultimate cheerleader and is always willing to share her divinely inspired gifts with the world. For every font suggestion, graphics review, website tweak and long tearful chat—I am grateful. Keisha is that friend who pushes just hard enough to make you a bit angry with her at times. She is the friend that sees your brilliance before you are willing to see it for yourself. Keisha is not afraid to offend you or make you uncomfortable if she knows that the challenge is necessary for you to step into your God-crafted purpose. She is a gift to many, and I am grateful for the hours she has given to help me get to this place in my journey. And then there is Barb. I could write a whole book about our relationship. She has been a boss, a mentor, a friend, an editor, a big sister, and an encourager. She, too, is willing to risk a possible conflict or altercation if that's what is needed to push you from victimhood to victor. She has allowed me to learn from her successes and her failures. She also made room for this book by forcing me to make room for myself.

Next, there is my family, which you already know is complicated. Ms. Elsie is my rock and, most certainly, "the wind beneath my wings." I could not have made it to the end of this book without her daily motivational emails, calls, and prayers. To my big brother Mark, whose own journey is an inspirational reminder to me that life is full of opportunities to pivot away from destructive behaviors and embrace abundance, to my younger siblings Louis, Timmy, and Melissa whom I met later in life, and the aunts and uncles who always have my back—you represent some of the kindest, funniest, most generous people I know. I am so grateful for your combined love and acceptance. And to my dad, Papa Bear, I miss you always. You taught me to tell a story and connect with others uniquely and intimately—thank you. But my family does not just consist of my brothers and sisters. God has uniquely chosen a family circle for me that I could never have imagined for myself. .

To my DeLatte loves, Lex and Ebo, my life would be empty without you. You have helped me to have fun, accepted me during my most unflattering seasons, and pushed me to pursue that which God has called me to. Words are inadequate to describe the love and admiration I have for you.

To my Liv, you are a rare and flashy gem! You inspire me to uncover my fierceness and always strive for excellence. You are the unoffendable friend—the one who leads with grace during times of chaos. The way you and Kevin share your children with Lenny and me helps to fill the unavoidable void that infertility has created. Coco and Carter James fill my heart with such joy. I am so grateful to call you family.

I can't mention family without acknowledging my second mom, Mima, my bestie Jerilee, and the entire Carney clan. I am alive to write this book because, during my darkest hours, you chose to intercede for me. You collectively held my head above the crashing waves of betrayal, cancer, and pain. Without reservation, you consistently stepped into my suffering and helped to bear the burdens that weighed me down. Your family is mine, and I am yours.

To my girls, Rebekah, Kate, Onika, Kennisha, Alla, Crystal, Nancy, and Georgia, you all have made this book possible because of your years of love, support, and encouragement. I treasure each of you.

To the men in my life, Mich, Brandon, and Michael. Thank you. Mich, you have picked up the slack and managed my life (and emotions) in ways that I cannot explain on paper. Your support made room for me to write. Brandon, you are that annoying yet totally wise and somewhat ridiculous little brother that God knew I needed. You have brought laughter and joy to the most miserable times of life, and I am incredibly grateful. To my Michael—oh, Michael. You supported me through cancer, career failures, divorce, more cancer, remarriage, and the list goes on. You were my bright light in the middle of the darkest moments. You are the definition of friendship, and the impact you've had on my life cannot be measured.

I cannot finish this book without mentioning those who have tended to my body and my soul. To my doctors, John and David, thank you. Thank you for being passionate about keeping me alive for such a time as this. Thank you for the sacrifices that you make every day so that many more people can live and not die. And to my church—my pastors, my choir, my community of faith—what would I do without you? I have no idea. Watching you worship, serve, and love will prove to be one of the highlights of my entire life. You fueled my faith when I was running on empty. Thank you for your attention and sacrifice of praise.

And now for Mr. Walker. There will never be enough words, or the right words. You are like that extra strong, luxurious lining that comes in super-expensive coats. You make even the coldest moments feel cozy while protecting me from the harsh elements of life. You handle my special version of "crazy" better than anyone else. Thank you for every dinner you cooked and every dish you washed so that I could focus and write. Thank you for always making sure that I had shampoo and toothpaste so that I also stayed presentable. And thank you for telling me it was time to shower when I lost track of the days. You continue to make me a better, more humble, kind, and organized person. I can never thank you enough for choosing to be my partner in life.

Lastly, I thank YOU. Thank you for going on this journey with me. Thank you for deciding to choose joy. Thank you for choosing to pivot toward hope so that your life can become a source of joy for others. Thank you for choosing to live for today with the hope of tomorrow. I am so grateful for the time you've taken to get to know me, and I hope to get to know you too someday.

With a heart full of joy and thanksgiving,

V